T0272577

EYES ON THE HORIZON

EYES ON THE HORIZON

My Journey Toward Justice

BALARAMA HOLNESS

HarperOne
An Imprint of HarperCollins*Publishers*

HarperCollins books may be purchased for educational, business, or sales promotional use. For information, please email the Special Markets Department in the U.S. at SPsales@harpercollins.com or in Canada at HCOrder@harpercollins.com.

FIRST EDITION

Designed by Bonni Leon-Berman

Library and Archives Canada Cataloguing in Publication information is available upon request.

ISBN 978-0-06-311195-0
ISBN 978-1-4434-6503-8 (Canada)

23 24 25 26 27 LBC 5 4 3 2 1

Dedicated to my daughter: Bella Angélique Holness

CONTENTS

ONE

THE SEEDS OF MY EXISTENCE

It was a cold November night in 1979. Frost covered the tinted windows of The Forum, the concert arena that was also home to the Montreal Canadiens hockey team.

Bob Marley and the Wailers' Survival Tour was the concert of the year, and Murielle and her friend Lise were lucky to have tickets. Twenty-three-year-old Murielle wore a loose-fitting white dress that fell just above her knees. The brown leather strap of her purse matched her well-worn boots. In her hand she gripped her ticket.

The venue was nearly full as they entered its cavernous main space and shimmied through the crowd to their seats at the back, where they were wedged between two men. One was with a group of friends. The other seemed to be alone.

"Allô, je suis Murielle," she said to her solo neighbor, her thick Quebecer accent blending in with the voices of the predominantly francophone concertgoers. The man looked at her and smiled, his brown eyes soft and kind. "I'm Bevin," he replied in English. "Cheers to a good show!" he added, while raising the drink in his hand. His nappy hair and suede vest, both black, complemented his light blue shirt and chocolate-colored skin. Lise and Murielle continued to make small talk with him in their broken English until the lights dimmed. People began to scream, raising their lighters in the air. Like a million fireflies, individual flames filled the now dark stadium with their warm glow as the stage lights began to flash in the band's signature Rastafarian colors—red, green, and gold.

Out of the darkness, Marley appeared, larger than life, his chiseled face standing in sharp contrast to his crown of thick, dark brown dreadlocks. The revolutionary musician who had conquered countries, not by force of arms, but through his conscientious music, began to cast his loving spell on the crowd.

As the band began to play, Murielle stood up and raised her arms in the air, her bracelets jangling to the rhythm of the mounting beat. Lise, always more reserved, stayed seated, tapping her foot to the music. As the rhythms engulfed the crowd, the smell of ganja filled the stadium.

As she urged her friend to join the dancing crowd, Murielle saw her neighbor jamming to the music. Without thinking, she grabbed his hand and raised it in the air with hers.

"This is the real thing!" he said, as he pulled her in close to make sure she could hear him. She felt the warmth of his breath on her ear. It gave her goose bumps. She looked up. Their faces just inches apart, they locked eyes. A bead of sweat dropped down Bevin's forehead. With their hands still intertwined, they swayed to the rhythm of the Wailers' heavy bass, rhythm guitar, and keyboards as Bob Marley's powerful voice blasted through speakers encircling the edge of the stage. In that moment, among a crowd of nearly eighteen thousand people, the seeds of my existence were sown.

..

My mother's and father's backgrounds couldn't have been more different. Bevin was a Jamaican, Murielle a Quebecer. He was a country boy, she a city slicker. He came from a well-to-do family, attended a prestigious private school in Jamaica, and then immigrated to Canada to complete his postsecondary education. She was born into a working-class family and went straight into the workforce as a secretary after high school. The list goes on and on.

I have always marveled at the way my parents, despite their differences, were drawn to each other. They've told me their connection that night was instantaneous. It's especially mystifying given that their identities so closely mirrored the larger social and political divisions in Quebec at the time. Francophone Quebecers viewed their language, culture, and ultimately their identity as distinct and under threat from anyone who was considered "other": anglophones, religious minorities, immigrants, and the global community at large.

Bevin immigrated to Montreal in 1969 to attend Sir George Williams University, which became Concordia University in 1974. It was a time of enormous political and social upheaval. Quebec was still in the midst of its "Quiet Revolution," or *Revolution tranquille*, which saw, among other things, the secularization of society away from the grip of the Catholic Church and the emergence of what would become the sovereignty movement. The previous year, journalist Pierre Vallières, a leader in the Front de libération du Québec (FLQ), had published his incendiary manifesto *Nègres blancs d'Amérique* (known in English as *White N———s of America*), which, comparing their plight to that of enslaved Blacks in the American South, called for French-Canadians to take up arms against their English oppressors. Violence was in the air. In Montreal, the FLQ had begun a series of bombings against anglophone targets that would culminate in the 1970 October Crisis, which saw the kidnapping of James Cross, a British diplomat, and the murder of Quebec cabinet minister Pierre Laporte. Inspired by the civil rights movement south of the border, the city was also becoming a magnet for Black activism. The year my father began attending courses at Sir George Williams, a sit-in at its downtown campus to protest the racist treatment of Black students turned into the largest student riot in Canadian history after police broke down the activists' barricades.

Montreal was very different from the sleepy, country town of Myersville, Saint Elizabeth, Jamaica, where my father was born and raised, and where his family still lived on their sprawling farm, chock-full of centennial mango trees, taller than Montreal's greystone townhomes.

The struggle for Quebec's independence had become a battle of identity politics: white francophones wanted to assert their claim as a distinct, sovereign nation, while the rest of the population, anglophones and immigrants especially, aimed to maintain their way of life within a united Canada.

Just months before Bevin and Murielle met, those tensions had reached a boiling point. The separatist movement, led by the governing Parti Québécois, had gained significant traction in the province. A referendum on whether Quebec should separate from the rest of Canada was on the horizon. My parents' identities may have reflected the linguistic, cultural, and sociopolitical divisions in Quebec society, but their love—at least for the time being—made such banal, worldly considerations seem trivial.

FOR MY MOTHER, THE RELATIONSHIP also offered a balm for personal trauma. In 1971, when she was only fifteen years old, her own mother had died while lying in my mother's lap as they rushed to the hospital. Kind-hearted Mariette suffered from severe depression, and her death was later deemed a suicide by poisoning. The shock of that loss, and the powerlessness my mother felt witnessing that death in such close proximity, never left her. It profoundly affected her sense of belonging, adequacy, and need for support. She felt, in a word, abandoned. Mariette had been the one to make breakfast, to ask Murielle about her day, to say goodnight before she went to sleep. After her death, nothing was the same. When Murielle met my father, she was still living in the same house in the francophone neighborhood of Rosemont where her mother had ended her life. Painful reminders of her were everywhere.

Years after meeting Bevin, my mother would also suffer the tragic loss of two of her brothers, one from cancer, the other from suicide. Despite an admirable drive to move forward with her life, Murielle would still be searching, decades later, for a sense of home.

Bevin, too, had his trials and tribulations. Born in 1948, his life began with the death of his twin brother. "No one knows what happened, or so they claim," he told me. His tone and manner suggested he felt betrayed, that medical personnel were somehow negligent and his family complicit in their silence. That first experience, of coming into the world amidst death and the darkness of mistrust, influenced my father's worldview and how he dealt with people. Music, books, and spirituality would become his escape.

After the concert, my father and mother went to a bar nearby for a drink. Although Bevin had been taking French night classes since he had arrived in Canada, they spoke in English. Murielle wanted him to feel comfortable. This was new for her. Until that point, she had viewed the English language as a threat to her and her family's rights as French-speaking people who embodied Quebecer culture and values. She told me that their connection was unspoken and profound. Here, finally, was someone who seemed to truly *see* her. It made her feel safe, validated.

BEFORE PARTING WAYS THAT NIGHT, Bevin and Murielle planned to meet the next weekend on Mount Royal, the mountain park in the middle of the city. Their rendezvous spot was the George-Étienne Cartier monument, a grey granite obelisk topped by the winged Goddess of Liberty and surrounded by four bronze-cast lions. The statement inscribed at its base, *Avant tout, soyons Canadiens* ("Above all, be Canadian"), had become, in the context of the province's fraught identity politics, controversial, to say the least.

My mother was amazed to see Bevin arriving at a run. When she commented on it, he told her that in his youth he'd been called the "fastest boy in all of Jamaica"; he'd won gold at the track-and-field national championships and nearly raced at the Olympics until an injury kept him out of contention.

They headed up the mountain to Montreal's famous lookout, where a few winter runners and locals were posing for pictures in front of the Montreal skyline. As they walked along, my mother couldn't help but notice the alternately concerned and frowning looks she was getting from a passerby. Bevin noticed too. Later, in the patisserie on Mont-Royal Street, where they warmed themselves over a drink, he broached the subject.

He explained to Murielle that the looks she'd been getting were something she'd have to get used to if they stayed together, that many people still thought Black and white shouldn't mix. He told her about his long-standing strategy: to simply ignore ignorant, racist people like the ones they'd seen, to refuse to give them the satisfaction of stooping to their level. His speech, delivered with characteristic articulateness, both impressed my mother and left her reeling.

As a white francophone living in Montreal, Murielle had never experienced racism firsthand. She was in many ways the poster child for Quebecer identity. She fit the mold perfectly, and it worked to her advantage. Although she grew up in an open-minded household, my mother never discussed race with her family, nor was she exposed to the history of slavery, Indigenous genocide, and horror of colonialism in school. In fact, she never thought about it. So although she was accepting, she was also largely unaware that the province and country she was living in was founded on racist and colonialist ideologies that still permeated nearly every facet of society.

She did understand oppression, though. Despite their majority in Quebec, francophones like my mother and her family had historically been subordinate—socially, culturally, and economically—to the English. At the time, anglophone males earned more than francophone males. And although this differential had narrowed from the previous decade, due in part to the provincial government's introduction of language laws in the late 1970s, a deep inequality still existed. Known colloquially as Bill 101, the Charter of the French Language, the 1977 law made French the province's only official language, and the only language to be used for business, commerce, and government. In 1979, the city's storefronts were full of ghostly marks where the English possessive apostrophe-s had been physically removed so that business signage would conform to the charter. No matter how trivial, the law left no stone uncovered in an attempt to ensure the primacy of the French language.

That afternoon, my mother sat listening to Bevin's words in silence as she tried to unpack what being in a biracial relationship would mean for her, and for him. When he was done, she told him she wanted to know everything about him. And so he told her.

My father, Bevin Holness, came from a well-off family in Jamaica. His mother was a teacher, his father a farmer who owned land—a lot of it, which served the family well financially. They had maids who cooked and cleaned for them and fieldworkers who tilled and sowed the soil. My father describes his childhood as if he were living in the Garden of Eden. The farm's beautiful dark red soil gave root to hundreds of mango trees. His father also raised goats, chickens, pigs, and cattle.

After he reluctantly retired from track following a serious quad injury, Bevin faced a decision about his life: Would he stay in Jamaica, or expand his horizons away from the island? It was painful. He loved his family deeply, but he had intellectual aspirations and couldn't imagine spending his entire life on a farm. So in 1969 he left for Montreal to attend university.

This surprised my mother, who, perhaps as a result of her own subconscious prejudices, hadn't expected him to be university educated. Murielle was working at a low-wage secretarial job and had no plans to go back to school. Now here was Bevin telling her about Canada's long history of colonialism, racism, and oppression, about how, in the ten years since his arrival, he had constantly been judged by his physical characteristics. "Canadians are polite and will greet you with kindness," she recalled him saying. "But if you're Black, you'll also be greeted with suspicion. Jamaica isn't like that. In Jamaica, a man is just a man."

He told her about a run-in he'd had with police not long after he'd arrived to Canada. It was morning, and he was on his way to a flea market to look for a few books. As he was standing on the corner, waiting to cross the street, he noticed a cop car slow down instead of continuing through the green light. He didn't think much of it, but just as he was heading into the market, he felt a tap on his back.

"Excuse me sir, I need to see your ID," the cop said in broken English, before continuing to pepper my father with questions. "Where are you from? Where do you live?" It was an immediate and aggressive interrogation. My father was not intimidated although the cop and his partner both carried holstered guns. My father reached in his pocket for his ID, but he didn't have it with him. "I don't have my ID," he told them. The police had been skeptical of my father and his intentions before that, but even more so now. Telling him he had to go with them, they handcuffed him and put him in the back of their patrol car. He felt like a criminal, even though he'd done nothing wrong.

At the station, he gave the police his details—name, age, address—so they could check their records. As they did, my father told them his story—that he'd studied science at Concordia University, that he currently worked in a laboratory. He said that his rights, and his dignity, were being infringed upon. His articulate manner of speaking seemed to change their opinion of him. Eventually, they let him go, no more questions asked.

My mother was confused. His mannerism, way of speaking, and overall behavior eventually made the cops change their minds. My father dissolved their biases of what a stereotypical Black was. His shocking response would, once again, stick with her: "Because I'm Black, Murielle, but I'm not a n———." Bevin actually had very conservative views on race and self-determination. Coming from an upper-class family in Jamaica, he'd always believed that holding oneself in a proper manner would override all forms of oppression.

His "lift yourself up by your bootstraps" ideology eventually faded. Over the years, my father would learn that all the self-determination in the world wasn't enough to protect his humanity and dignity. Racism in Quebec was pervasive. From housing discrimination to racial profiling, he would come to know what it was like to be a Black man—in a Western country. Racism creates oppression, but it also creates mystic-like, fiery rebels and revolutionaries with the ability to transform evil into optimism, change, and humanity. When my parents met, their alchemy created exactly that.

MY MOTHER HAD NEVER MET ANYONE who spoke with the clarity, conviction, and self-assuredness that Bevin did. He was brilliant, and she was in awe.

They quickly grew intimate. Murielle shared many details of her life with him, including the seven-inch-long scar that ran vertically down her abdomen, the result of a car accident she'd been in just a few years prior. She and her boyfriend had been high. He suffered a broken leg, but Murielle had lost her spleen. She told him how, a few months before the crash, the cops had caught her and the same boyfriend hotboxing in an empty parking lot in the Old Port and had written them up. How the car accident, although unfortunate, was a wakeup call to change her habits and distance herself from bad company.

But she held off talking about what had happened to her mother five years before, and about her lingering trauma. The wounds still felt fresh. But she knew their relationship wouldn't progress unless she opened up to him completely. So the following summer, on another of their walks on the mountain, she finally broached the subject.

She talked about how my grandmother's mental health struggles and decision to end her life continued to reverberate through her family. At the time of her death, Quebec had one of the highest rates of suicide in the nation, nearly one hundred each month. It was a real, but unspoken, epidemic.

On a frigid day in January of 1980, he asked Murielle to meet him at Berri metro station. He told her he wanted to take her somewhere that was special to him, though he wouldn't tell her what or where it was. It was the first time in their brief relationship that my mother had felt uneasy, but he assured her she could trust him.

After exiting the metro at Pie-IX station, Bevin lead Murielle down Pie-IX Boulevard. After a ten-minute walk, he pointed to a large brownstone building. To my mother, it looked a lot like a church. She was confused, and a tad unimpressed. He acknowledged that the building was an old Protestant church but told her not to judge a book by its cover.

As they stepped inside, my mother's eyes widened. She saw white walls adorned with colorful streamers and flower garlands, stained-glass windows bordered by intricate gold filigree. Kirtan music played in the background, and the air smelled like carnations and jasmine. Women dressed in the most beautiful saris she had ever seen kneeled on the floor of what was clearly a Hindu temple. Chandeliers, lit by candles instead of light bulbs, hung from the ceiling. To my mother it felt like a movie, not real life.

She was worried about interrupting the ceremony in progress, but my father quickly guided her farther inside, where a man wearing a thick beige robe folded diagonally across his chest greeted them.

"Bakti! We've missed you these last few weeks," the man said as he reached out his hand to shake my father's. Bakti, Bevin explained to my mother, was the spiritual name given to him by the swamis.

Bevin introduced the man, who was a swami, to my mother, who was now much more at ease. But she was also flabbergasted. My father had never mentioned anything to her about being Hindu. It also didn't fit with the stories he'd told her about his devout, churchgoing family back in Jamaica.

The swami invited Bevin to show Murielle the rest of the temple, so they slipped off their shoes, a sign of cleanliness and respect in the Hindu tradition. Bevin told my mother that he came here nearly every day to pray, and meditate. He told her he was guided by God, and that he was at peace in life in general. Murielle couldn't help but notice how Bevin's disposition had changed the moment they arrived at the temple. He still seemed strong and confident, but his demeanor was softer and more introspective.

"The way I feel when I'm here is how I want you to feel forever," he told her. "You are safe here. You are safe with me. Let this temple be your refuge. Let my heart be your home." With those words, my father changed my mother's life forever. She fell in love.

ON APRIL 11, 1981, one and a half years after they had met at that Bob Marley concert, my parents married in a small ceremony in Montreal, surrounded by their loved ones and friends. It was exactly the way they wanted it to be: spiritual, loving, and freeing for them both.

Just two years later, my mother gave birth to me and my twin brother on July 20, 1983. My father, wanting my mother to feel at ease, had decorated her room at the Royal Victoria Hospital like the temple that they both attended. He placed candles on the windowsills and garlands across the edges of the bed frame. The solace that my father, and his spirituality, brought to her during her pregnancy and the birth strengthened their bond as never before.

My parents were elated when my brother and I were born

healthy and strong. Losing his own twin brother at birth had made my father worry about the birth of his own twins. To my parents, we were a miracle. My mother always told me that motherhood was a blessing in and of itself. My brother and I had given her a chance to be the rock her own mother hadn't been able to be, at least not for long. It was the beginning of a new chapter, one my parents welcomed with open arms, open hearts, and open minds.

They named us Balarama Das Holness and Jagannatha Das Holness, after Hindu gods, to embody the inner peace and strength they had gained from what, for my mother, was a newfound spirituality. We were the manifestation of hours of prayer, meditation, and love. The rare alchemy that connected my parents to each other—one that went beyond citizenship, race, ethnicity, religion, and language—was the basis of my existence. In their bond, too, I found my life's mission: to erase social divisions, just like Bob Marley did on that infamous evening in 1979.

TWO

THE ASHRAM

The Hindu philosophy and way of life that my father introduced Murielle to set her on a path of growth, healing, and spirituality. She embraced it completely. But as much as the birth of me and my brother brought her joy, our mother still grappled with the pain and emptiness associated with losing her own mother. The challenges of marriage and having twins would soon begin to take a toll on her, and Bevin as well. They started arguing, and the more they did so, the more my mother realized that the bond she had with my father, like all things in life, was ephemeral. Marital tension exposed and exacerbated their differences. Initially, she'd been drawn to my father because he seemed to offer a life beyond the limited one she was living on the east side of Montreal. He helped bring out her true nature, which was restless and adventurous, optimistic and ambitious. Over time, though, she came to see Bevin as stagnant; a bookish man stuck in his intellectual bubble—someone who could precisely detail how to build a fortress but wouldn't budge to move a brick.

My father abandoned the science work, and took odd jobs here and there. Eventually, he decided to work for himself. At one point, he bought a large blue van and started buying and selling merchandise at a flea market. Despite the nominal income, as far as he was concerned, it was worth it. For him, being told what to do, having his time and life controlled by someone else, was intolerable. Most of all, he did enough to provide us with the basics, especially love and attention.

My father was more interested in pursuing a pious life, dedicated to God, than he was in pursing the endless rat race. Though his family had attended church every Sunday in Jamaica, he still had questions that no one seemed to be able to answer. As a young churchgoer, he had always wondered, when the priest said "the Father, the Son, and the Holy Spirit," who that father was. That question never left him. It was only when he came to Canada that he finally found what he was looking for, at the Hindu temple.

In my mother's view, my father had become a sidenote in the household, despite his instinctual nurturing of us. As she nursed Jugy, as we called my twin brother, and me to sleep in her arms, she came to believe that she was all we needed. She would not allow her husband's flaws to slow her down. She wanted to take on the world, be the architect of her own universe. My mother's independence surely influenced my father's view of women. When I got older, he would tell me, in an assertive tone, that "as soon as a woman has children, she dismisses the man because she no longer needs him."

For Murielle, the temple provided an opportunity to elevate her journey beyond what my father could provide. She found there a deep sense of solace, arrival, and peace. And so when she was presented with the opportunity to take her spirituality to the next level by moving to New Vrindaban, a holy Hindu community tucked in the hills of West Virginia, she seized it. She had heard stories of New Vrindaban and had been beguiled by the values it represented and the life that it could offer her—and us. To my mother, New Vrindaban promised the ultimate adventure, one far away from

Montreal, site of her past trauma, her mundane day-to-day life, and her increasingly unhappy marriage.

Without filing for a divorce, my mother told Bevin that she was leaving with Jugy and me, not yet one year old, for a place she had never even visited. My father underestimated my mother's decisiveness. He didn't think she would leave and figured that if she did, she would return after a few weeks. My mother, though, having come out of her shell, was craving adventure, a way to escape her past while discovering the world beyond Montreal. Once she made her choice and set her sights on the horizon beyond my father, there was no going back. One cool June morning in 1984, our lives changed forever. With only a few suitcases of belongings, my mother, brother, and I set off for New Vrindaban. Murielle had asked her brother Bob to chauffer us on the fourteen-hour drive, which he did without hesitation.

Although for years I viewed my parents' brief connection as an act of God, I now see it in another way as well, namely, as a spiritual bond that at first enabled healing and personal growth. When they met, both were broken in some way, shaken by death in their respective families. Spirituality and love brought them together, but while this numbed their individual pain, it also put them on divergent paths. For my father, healing required stability and, to a certain extent, solitude, which was hard to find with a new, young family. For my mother, healing required rediscovering her joie de vivre. She couldn't find that joy in Montreal with my father and mundane life in the city. And so she departed on a wild, life-changing adventure to New Vrindaban.

A PALACE OF GOLD. A TEMPLE. Clouds of burning incense. Statues of deities carved from dark grey stone. A long, wood-paneled dining hall filled with the aroma of curry, coriander, and garam masala. Outside the temple, small cabins and mobile homes dotted more than a hundred acres of utopian farmland edging the majestic Appalachian Mountains. There were meandering creeks, peaceful ponds, and barns where cows were bred for milk, butter, and ghee. A melting pot of cultures and identities. The Hindu faith, of course, figured centrally, but there were also those with Baptist values and Indigenous ways of being. Christian holidays were celebrated. From when I was one year old, New Vrindaban was my home, my community, and my playground—the place where I first came to consciousness and where my childhood memories begin.

Located in Marshall County, a sleepy blue-collar enclave in northern West Virginia, New Vrindaban epitomized rural living, albeit with a spiritual twist. Here was an austere lifestyle vastly different from materialistic, fast-paced Montreal. Costs were low, culture was rich, and community was strong. The philosophy in New Vrindaban, which had already been around for nearly twenty years when we arrived there, was simple: no meat eating, no illicit sex, no intoxication, and no gambling. It also was home to South Asian, Black, and Indigenous people who, just over one hundred years before, would have been enslaved or indentured on these same lands. Lewis Wetzel, a famous "Indian fighter" who participated in several military campaigns against Native American peoples in the area, was buried at the edge of the ashram. In Marshall County, he was hailed as a "legendary frontier scout"—the words are even carved into his headstone.

For Jugy and me, living in the ashram meant being raised with Hindu influences, culture, and traditions. We were so immersed that my first word was "Mata," Sanskrit for "Mom." (Eventually I learned that "Pita" was "Father," though my father would not be present in my life for nearly a decade.) My upbringing was vastly different from my mother's, and from a typical one in the place where I was born.

Those differences included notions about the nature of family itself. When my brother and I were three years old, Mata spent long days raising money for the Hindu community. She quickly became the top earner, which meant spending significant amounts of time away from us. Despite her success, we lived modestly on the outskirts of the ashram in a two-bedroom cabin with a small kitchen. Occasionally, she'd take us on day trips to the city of Moundsville.

Dressed in traditional salmon-colored Hindu robes made from linen and delicate cotton thread, we always intrigued passersby, a majority of whom were working-class white folks who most likely had never seen or interacted with people so different from themselves. To them, we were misguided outcasts. To us, they were ignorant "karmies"—people who suffered from "spiritual malnutrition," who lived in ignorance, who were caught up in a rat race, unaware of the bad karma they were accumulating because of the greedy and lustful desires that led them to slaughter and eat animals, gamble, and get intoxicated. I distinctly remember asking Mata why the city kids looked so happy when they ate hamburgers from the local fast-food chains.

"Ignorance is bliss," she responded with a chuckle, and in so doing told me everything I needed to know. Connected to nature, conscious of the world around me, I was on a journey in which I was fortified by a spiritual nourishment that equipped me to interact with the universe in my own unique way.

Our family day trips were rare in comparison to the longer fund-raising trips my mother took away from the ashram without us. At first she left us weekly, then biweekly, then every other day. Although Jugy and I were still very young, it felt, at times, like she was more attached to the road than to us. Soon, we hardly saw her; our neighbors and teachers became our stand-in parents.

When Jugy and I were five years old, shortly before we were to start school for the first time, I was awoken at night by a series of sounds: the clacking of Mata's shoes on the kitchen's wooden floor, the soft jingling of her house keys, and the rustling of what I knew was the blue-and-white windbreaker she'd brought with her from Montreal when we first moved to the ashram. As I heard the whisper of wind that signaled the front door closing, I knew Mata was about to leave us, again. Although there was nothing new about her making a getaway in the middle of the night, when she assumed we were asleep, this time it felt different. I felt like I was being abandoned.

As I tore out of the cabin in my dark blue pajamas, I caught sight of the rear bumper of her car as it disappeared in the dust of the gravel road. Despite the tears clouding my vision, I ran as fast as I could toward the car.

"Mata, stop!" I shouted. "Come back!" I shouted again, my chest pounding and lungs aching. Balarama, my name, means omnipotent power, so I thought I could make her turn around. But running my fastest and shouting my loudest weren't enough. I was defeated, and it hurt.

Though episodes like this would recur over the next few years, Mata became better at escaping before we woke up, having already arranged for a neighbor or guardian upon her departure, or simply stopped coming home altogether. The hurt of these abandonments eventually hardened to conscious and subconscious scars. Mata's trips grew longer and longer, to the degree that, between the ages of seven and ten, I have little to no recollection of her at all. Our prime connection was through letters and gifts in the mail. It could be that at a certain point she decided it would cause us more pain to come back to us for short periods of time, so she simply ceased doing so. It didn't matter to Jugy and me that she was one of the top fund-raisers for our Hindu community. All we knew was that our mother wasn't there for us.

Being so young, we were also unaware of her personal struggles, of the pain and loss that she had experienced from a young age, and of the loneliness she must have felt deep within her soul. Our community, her job, and the Hindu faith fulfilled her on one level, and yet there was always something missing. Her restless search for that something, I would realize years later, was what hampered her ability to provide the stability Jugy and I so desperately needed.

Although it had been fifteen years since she had lost her mother, for Mata the agony never disappeared. Her adventures, projects, even her love for Pita, all convinced her, temporarily, that she was happy. Perhaps if she had addressed the root causes of her pain, instead of fleeing from them, things might have been different. But she was afraid to confront the demons of her past and scared of what might resurface, so she hid behind her trips, her fund-raising goals, and her faith. The ashram was the ultimate escape—a community that would revere her dedication rather than see it for what it was: a way to reorient focus away from her sadness and toward a "greater good." I'm not suggesting Mata's work wasn't admirable or selfless (because it most definitely was), only that it served her as much as she served it. By moving to the ashram, she not only satisfied her desire for adventure and escape, but she gained a community that accepted her, unconditionally, and that, unlike her mother, would be there for her permanently or so she thought. The ashram provided both stability and freedom, but the latter came at a cost: her relationship with her children.

Mata's free spirit and curiosity lured her away from a routine, mundane life. Which didn't mean she didn't love us. She always made sure we were safe, built us a community at the ashram, and gave us the independence, responsibility, and trust that we needed to thrive. At the end of the day, she gave us the greatest gift of all—an understanding of love as a force that could traverse geographical and cultural lines, that didn't depend on labels or conventions. But the constant departures and long absences did erode our bond. At a certain point, I could no longer trust that Mata would be there for us. This affected my behavior later in life: I did not trust people in general. In relationships I rarely ever said "I love you." Why would I? It would end and they would leave anyways, so I may as well leave before they did. Whenever I felt crossed by someone, I would find it hard to forgive that person, or accept them back into my life. I may have forgiven my mother, but in many ways, the scars still remain.

BEING RAISED BY OTHER FAMILIES at the ashram, Jugy and I grew accustomed to always having a support system, albeit one that didn't include our mother or father. Although, being twins, we were the same age, Jugy had always been wiser and stronger than me. In the absence of our parents, it was Jugy I looked up to; in many ways, he was my entire world. Although Mata would come and go, Jugy and I always knew we had each other.

Our days at the ashram centered around going to school, meditating in the temple, and playing in the pastures with our friends. On the evenings when she was home, Mata would prepare us a simple meal, usually basmati rice and *sabji* (a mix of vegetables and Indian spices). I can still hear the beautiful, soft tune she would whistle as she cooked in the kitchen.

One night at the dinner table, when we were about five or six years old, Jugy and I were being rowdy, loud, and outspoken. Maybe we were just tired of asking Mata to stay and figured that our boisterous behavior would cover that up, or at least get us some attention. In what was no doubt a bit of rebellion and angst, Jugy threw his pita on the floor. The vegetables slid across the wood floor, leaving a trail of brown marinade behind them. In a series of swift and decisive movements, Mata got up, pushed in her chair, picked up Jugy's pita, and threw it back on his plate. Standing behind him, she grabbed the side of his head and pushed it into the food in front of him. I was shocked. Within seconds, I got up from my seat and jumped on her back.

"Don't touch my brother!" I yelled as loudly as I could. Shaking me off, Mata turned around, looked at me with sunken eyes, and, without saying a word, darted to her bedroom at the end of the hallway. My heart was pounding, as I'm sure Jugy's was too. But we sat in silence. We waited for Mata to come back into the kitchen. We called her, but she didn't come.

I slowly approached her room. Then, placing my hand on the frame for support, I opened the door slightly and peered through the crack. She was sitting on the edge of her bed, the long skirt of her sari nearly touching the floor. Her hands were clasped tightly as tears rolled down her cheeks. I knew then that Mata was hurt, but I didn't know how to deal with her sorrow.

"Mata?" I said, quietly. "Can I have an apple?"

"Yes, take one from the fridge," she answered, her voice cracking as she momentarily tried to hold back her tears. I felt I needed to ask permission to eat, despite being in my own home. I had learned my manners from other families, and constantly being in someone else's care meant always having to ask for what I wanted or needed.

We never spoke about the incident again. No apologies. No fights. No tears. Just silence. But I think it was the first time *all of us* realized just how disconnected and broken our little family was. Talking about it was too difficult. But the silence between us grew louder as Mata's fund-raising trips grew longer. Jugy and I eventually moved in with our schoolteacher, Manancy, an Indian woman who had two sons, Dave and Sham.

The brown shag carpet that lined Manancy's long house made it feel cozy and warm, as did the smell of warm chai brewing on the stove. We loved it. We felt safe. We felt cared for. Dave and Sham became our best friends and Manancy our second mom. It was as if we'd gotten a new lease on life—one that we cherished. Jugy and I were happy.

We never thought about Pita, our father, because he was never there. The one time he came to visit us at the ashram he was greeted with hostility, my mother and the swamis fearing that he would take us back to Canada. We had come to New Vrindaban without his consent and had been living illegally in the United States for years. Years later, my father told me that on that visit I called him "Ravana"—one of the main antagonists in an infamous Hindu story. I held disdain for Pita without even realizing it.

AUSTERITY, DISCIPLINE, AND A KEEN SENSE of responsibility were drilled into us by both Manancy and the ashram's swamis. Beginning around age seven, we were expected to rise at 5:30 each morning, take a cold shower, prepare fresh butter, or clean the barns. After completing our morning tasks, we would head to the temple for morning prayers, where we'd sit near the back, cross-legged, on the warm wooden floor. On special occasions, we'd be asked to pick marigolds from the gardens to adorn the temple's altars, and our hands and clothes would smell of beautiful floral perfume throughout the prayer ceremony. At our school, which was on the community grounds, we were taught by community leaders who used a modified, student-centered version of the state curriculum to encourage exploration of our surroundings. We learned about nature, and life, by building tree houses and birdhouses, or analyzing different types of plants. Our schooling was connected to our morning chores, the temple, our homes, and the community.

When we celebrated Hindu festivals, the community was awash in color, music, and joy. Magenta, violet, and orange flower garlands would adorn the ashram's gravel pathways, gold-leafed altars, and dark, wooden tables. Beautiful music would fill the air, compelling people to dance and sing along with traditional Hindu songs. I remember sitting on the steps of the temple, clutching paper plates piled high with coconut and mango and plastic cups filled with soft, spongy gulab jamuns, waiting to watch the intricate fireworks display. As the harmonium played inside the temple, pops of red, white, and gold would blaze overhead, turning the darkness into a bright, heavenly spectacle. The next morning, we'd run through the fields looking for unexploded fireworks.

Though we had respect for the Hindu faith and for the beautiful utopia we were living in, Jugy and I were also rebelliously mischievous young boys. Egged on by our friends, we would swing from vines and wade through creeks, catching tadpoles, frogs, and salamanders. We'd dream up our own games and climb the tall walnuts and sugar maples scattered around the ashram. We roughhoused and got into fights when we played soccer, basketball, and football—the latter being our favorite pastime.

In the summer months, we would frequent Swan Lake—a reservoir just down the road from the temple surrounded by lush green grass, tall trees, and beautiful wood cabanas with copper-colored roofs. There, I would watch the older kids climb to the top of the cabanas and jump into the lake, which we all called the ghat. The splashing sound as they hit the water always intrigued me. But I tended to timidly watch instead of joining in the fun. That is, until Jugy decided to take the leap as well.

"Come on Bala, let's try," he said, waving his hand to beckon me over from the bank to the cabana. "It looks fun!"

"Jugy, I don't know how!" I yelled, but he didn't look back.

I watched in awe as he climbed the side of the cabana without any hesitation. Within seconds, he was in the air, arms flailing as he flew above the ghat and then disappeared into its cold, teal-colored water. I waited for what seemed like an eternity, but couldn't see Jugy. I was scared something had happened to him. Then, all of a sudden, he emerged from the depths and swam quickly toward me.

"Bala, you have to try! It's so much fun!" Jugy was always more courageous than me—willing to take risks, albeit calculated ones. Seeing the smile on his face as he climbed out of the water made me want to jump too, but it would be nearly two weeks before I mustered up the courage.

"I'll only do it if you come with me," I said to Jugy one hot day in mid-August. "I need your help." Without hesitation, Jugy and I put on our matching grey swim trunks and ran to the ghat, our bare feet leaving imprints in the grass path that stretched from Manancy's house to the lake.

"You can do it, Bala!" Jugy yelled encouragingly as we reached the peak of the cabana. I looked into Jugy's eyes and gripped his hand. Jugy was my protector, my savior, my safety net. I loved him and I loved our bond. If he was with me, I felt like I could do anything.

"One, two, three, cannonball!" I yelled as we jumped into the ghat together.

ON SUNDAYS, WE WOULD GATHER around the ashram's sole television set to watch NFL games. Although I didn't have the patience to sit through the full broadcast, I became deeply fascinated with Jim Kelly, Bruce Smith, and Andre Reed, players from my favorite team, the Buffalo Bills. Other than football, we didn't get a lot of exposure to "traditional" entertainment. In fact, until I was nine years old, I had seen only two movies: *The Ten Commandments* and *Ben-Hur*. *The Ten Commandments* had an especially significant impact on me, forming my childhood understanding of good and evil. It was easy for me to grasp that if God were on your side, anything was possible, from freeing slaves to parting the Red Sea.

The only other time I watched television, ironically, was in school. When we turned seven, most of us ashram kids were obliged—for reasons beyond our understanding—to attend Limestone Elementary, a state school fifteen minutes away by car and unaffiliated with the Hindu community. On my first day, after entering the classroom and sitting in my assigned seat, I recall the principal's voice booming over the loudspeaker to give us the daily news and school updates. After the announcements ended, our teacher asked us to stand and place our hands on our chests. I looked at Jugy and Sham. We were all confused about what was going on, especially when the rest of the students, led by our teacher, began reciting what we thought was a poem.

"I pledge allegiance to the flag of the United States of America, and to the Republic for which it stands, one nation under God, indivisible, with liberty and justice for all." My eyes darted around the room. Why were we worshipping a country instead of God?

This was my first experience with people who didn't share the same faith as me, who lived a vastly different life from mine, and who obeyed state rules instead of religious tenets. It was at Limestone where I first began to understand the difference between human-made and natural law. Living at the ashram, Jugy and I weren't subject to the same rules that the Limestone kids were. We were steeped in nature, in religion, and in spirituality. We knew what it meant to be free—running through the rolling foothills of the Appalachian Mountains, praying in some of the world's most beautiful temples, and living outside of state institutions that demanded conformity to their ideals. The Limestone kids were clearly different from us ashram kids. They craved structure. We craved self-determination, autonomy, individualism, and self-sufficiency.

As a child, I didn't understand the intricacies of the American concept of freedom. And I wouldn't have, based on my experience at Limestone. Freedom is meant to be emancipatory, but the institutions that governed my karmie classmates' lives seemed to stifle their ability to act and think freely, to challenge the rules that were imposed on them from birth. This unquestioning acceptance of "American freedom," which in many ways I viewed (and still do) as being inadequate, made the word "freedom" itself seem distant, and essentially meaningless to me. The way I see it, self-determination, outspokenness, and unconformity are necessary parts of what it means to be truly free.

Perhaps this is why, decades after I left Limestone and the ashram, I felt comfortable challenging the norms of the society I lived in, living on my own terms, and breaking social, cultural, and archaic political molds. It was ironically in this way that Limestone—a rigid state school that encouraged conformity—set me free.

I FELT CONNECTED TO THE HINDU FAITH from a young age, and my spirituality was evident to nearly all the swamis at the ashram. Once, a head swami asked to read my birth charts. After flicking through the dog-eared pages of his Indian astrology books, and then looking back up at me, the swami placed his hand on mine, his warmth radiating onto my skin.

"By your fortieth birthday, you will have become a guru," he said. His tone—low, steady, and reassuring—gave me the sense that he was not only serious, but that I had an important duty and responsibility to uphold his prediction. I wasn't sure, though, what a guru was. Too afraid to ask the swami, I waited until Mata was back from one of her fund-raising trips to ask her about the interaction.

"Mata, what's a guru?" I said, looking up at her kind, blue eyes.

"They're leaders and teachers who help guide people," she replied, without asking me why I wanted to know. Maybe she felt my energy, my duty, my responsibility. She was, after all, deeply connected to the faith.

I was immersed in thought for the rest of the night. Both Mata's and the swami's prophetic words had an enormous impact on me. I began to believe that I could do great things. It was an early vote of confidence that gave me purpose.

From that day on, I took part in as many spiritual ceremonies and rituals as I could, trying to soak in my surroundings. When I turned eight, I was finally allowed to join in on the sweat lodge, a practice that, along with the burning of sage and other typically Indigenous cultural practices, had become adopted by and deeply embedded in the community. The swamis who conducted the ceremony—so noble, wise, understanding, and intentional—were revered in the ashram. I wanted to emulate them, and in so doing, be respected. I saw my initiation into the sweat lodge as a ticket upward.

Being the boisterous risk-taker that I was, I raced into the lodge—a large, green circular hut whose entrance was covered by a large flap—as soon as I was given the go-ahead. No preparation. No instruction. Just pure instinct and motivation. I felt like I was accelerating on my path to growth, development, and even enlightenment. Once everyone had entered, the flap was closed, leaving us in complete darkness as the swamis began throwing herbs and water onto the hot stones in the center. As the scent of burnt sage filled the air, the heat began to rise, filling my lungs to the point that I thought they might burst. As twin feelings of fear and panic jolted through me, I thought I was going to faint. I couldn't climb over the hot rocks. I was too far away from the exit to quickly escape. But I was also determined not to back down from the spiritual challenge in front of me. Reaching a new level of spirituality required sacrifice, concentration, inner fortitude, trust, and dedication. Looking back, it was a lot for an eight-year-old to ask of himself. I knew this would be a defining moment for me, and that, like the others I was sharing this experience with, I needed to look inward, meditate, and calm my nerves.

Taking a series of deep breaths, I began to accept the pain I felt. Repeating the mantras I'd grown up chanting each morning, my fears began to fade. And in that moment, I realized that my mind was my strongest weapon. My thoughts had the ability to empower me, and I needed to harness that power for good.

WHEN JUGY AND I WERE NINE YEARS OLD, a swami approached us just as afternoon prayer time was ending. We had been making noise with our friends close to the exit of the temple, so we assumed he was coming to ask us to quiet down. Instead, with a stoic face and tender hand, he asked Jugy and me to follow him into the temple's hallway. Jugy gripped my hand as the swami made small talk with us.

"Your Mata has been stopped at the border. She's not allowed back here," he told us. Although I'd heard what he said, its consequences didn't register in my mind, or in Jugy's. Mata spent so much time away from us that her absence was normal. We'd been taught in the temple that adverse situations like our mother's absence, or any situation or event for that matter, were "acts of God," and because I had faith, I trusted that this was part of my life journey. I was calm. I had no idea what this meant for her, or that a major change was in front of us.

Later that day, Jugy and I went back to Manancy's and told her the news.

"What!?" she cried in disbelief. She proceeded to eat the rest of her dinner in silence. It wasn't until I saw and heard Manancy's reaction that the weight of the news began to sink in. Mata was not coming back. Ever. What would happen to us? To our life at the ashram? After dinner, I went to the room that Jugy and I shared and sat on my bunk bed, seeking a refuge from the shock I felt. Sham must have heard my deep sighs from the living room, because he came in and plopped down next to me.

"You don't have to go to Canada," he said. "Anyways, they all live in igloos there!" I burst into laughter.

"I know, right? I'm going to freeze to death!" As our joking died down, I stared at the brown carpet in front of me, the smile on my face fading.

"But Mata is there, Sham. I miss her." I tried to stop the tears welling in my eyes. I had never cried in front of Sham before, but I was unable to stop myself: drip, drip, drip. The first teardrops hit the comforter in a damp, unpredictable pattern. I rubbed my eyes.

"I miss Mata," I said again, and burst into noisy tears. It all seemed overwhelming.

THE NEXT DAY, MANANCY, JUGY, AND I met with the head swamis. They had booked me and Jugy a flight to Montreal in just a couple days. We would be leaving the ashram for good. Jugy, unfazed by the news, jumped from his seat, "Wow, a plane ride! This is going to be so cool!" As I listened to him talk about all the things we could do on the plane, I felt better about the move. If Jugy was excited, I should be too. If he was with me, I would be fine.

Two days later, after packing what we could in the suitcases the swami had given us, we were driven to the airport by Manancy, with Sham and Dave coming along for the ride. Manancy spoke with the agent at the check-in counter to confirm our custody with the airline.

"Don't be afraid," Manancy whispered as she kissed us both on the tops of our heads. Her hand, resting on my shoulder, was warm and comforting. "You'll be with Mata soon."

The thing is, we weren't afraid at all. We were leaving the ashram, just like Mata had done for years. It didn't seem like a big deal. Manancy, Dave, Sham, and the swamis were more upset than we were. It wasn't because we didn't love them; we simply thought we would be back. Little did we know it was the last time we would see any of them.

As we waited in the airport to board our flight, we quietly observed our surroundings, jumping out of our seats when a gigantic plane rolled by the sky-high windows.

Jugy and I ran to board the flight ahead of the rest of the passengers. Suddenly, what was happening felt all too real, like my first jump into the ghat, when I was unsure whether I'd rise to the surface. Once again, I was jumping into the unknown.

The flight attendants seated us near the front of the aircraft and paid special attention to us. They knew it was our first time on an airplane and told us what to expect.

The almost five-hundred-mile trip took only an hour and a half. Jugy got the window seat, so I wrestled with him for a view of the magnificent winter scenery and diverse terrain below us: the forests and steep, rocky, winding mountains of Pennsylvania and the lowlands and small towns of New York. Like birds in the sky, flying to our new/old home to see our mother, we peered down at things on the ground that were the size of ants. We were going back to our birthplace, our true hometown, to be reunited with our mother—a bond that had been neglected, but was still there. We believed that this adventure was the start of something special.

THREE

WELCOME TO CANADA

Montreal's airport was like a portal into a new world. Gone were the green rolling hills, rose gardens, and lotus ponds of my childhood. I was about to encounter a new language, a new culture, and a new way of being and living. I didn't know what to expect, especially given that I had been separated from my mother for nearly three years. But Jugy was with me, and that gave me comfort.

One of the wheels of our dark grey suitcase was broken, and it squeaked as we exited the baggage claim area after going through customs, holding hands. Before we had even laid eyes on her, Mata's excited voice pierced through the dense crowd.

"Bala! Jugy!" Her hair, cut into a bob, was shorter and darker than I remembered. Hitting just below her cheekbones, it accentuated her smile as she greeted us.

"I've missed you so much," Mata whispered as she hugged us tightly. Her voice cracked and tears fell from her eyes, dripping onto my hair. "I missed you too!" we both replied at the same time. In the short span of time since we'd left the ashram, I'd already had so many conflicting feelings. At times I felt invincible and excited for change. At others, I felt like my world was crumbling in front of me and I had no agency to control it.

Later, we learned that Mata had worked for years to raise the money to establish a meditation center in Montreal called Serenity and Awakening—a spiritual refuge like the ashram we had grown up in. As an adult, I often wondered why she never told us about these plans, why she didn't take us with her, why she left us without explanation, and why, in our final years at the ashram, she barely visited us at all. Maybe she figured we were safer, more stable in the community with Manancy. Maybe she was protecting us from a life on the go. Or maybe she just felt she couldn't juggle the responsibility of her work with two young children. Sadly, I never got a chance to ask her. Regardless of my doubts or fears about the move, deep within my heart I craved love and affection from Mata, and landing in Montreal seemed like a first step toward rebuilding our relationship. I was full of hope.

Mata put our suitcases into the trunk of her ten-year-old blue Toyota Tercel, and we climbed in the back. Forty minutes later, after driving along the busy highway, then through the snow-filled February streets, we approached the corner of Saint-Denis and Beaubien. Mata gestured to the façade of a brown-brick duplex with exterior metal stairs. "Welcome home, boys," she said. In comparison to the ashram's cozy wooden cabins and mobile homes, it was huge. On the second-story balcony, a woman in her seventies or eighties stood smoking a cigarette. There was no front lawn or garden. As we turned the corner, we saw brown plastic garbage bins lining the side of the building. Mata parked in the alley—or, as I would soon come to know it, the *ruelle*—out back.

Jugy and I were momentarily speechless, but suddenly I found my words. "Home?" I said, before Jugy could get a word in. "This is where karmies are. This isn't where we're supposed to live." I was already experiencing culture shock. Yes, I was with Mata and Jugy, but I still felt out of place. Though I'd seen my new home only briefly, from a car window, I could tell it was a very different place from the spiritual one where I'd grown up.

"Spirituality lives within you, Bala. It isn't about your surroundings," Mata said. With a smile on her face, she got out of the car and opened the back door for us.

"Let me show you your new room. I think you'll like it," she said, placing her gloved hand on Jugy's shoulder to nudge him out of the car. I followed closely behind. As soon as Mata unlocked the door, we ran inside. The apartment was on the ground floor and looked very different from Manancy's house. Laid out along a single, long hallway, it had exposed brick walls and wood floors instead of carpeting. Its front windows let in a beam of light that reflected off a metal boot rack in the foyer. From there, we could see right through to the back wall of the apartment, where a beautifully framed photograph of a Hindu guru was hung. The home seemed warm and comforting.

Mata's devotion meant we would remain connected to our Hindu spirituality, despite living in a predominantly Christian province, city, and neighborhood. Montreal was founded by two devout Catholics—Paul de Chomedey de Maisonneuve and Jeanne Mance—who, in 1643, erected a cross at the top of Mount Royal that looms over the city to this day (the original wooden cross having long been replaced by one made of fabricated steel and LED lights). As a child, I didn't quite understand the differences between religions. The ashram was predominantly Hindu, but it was also an oasis of tolerance and acceptance where other practices were embraced. I remember there being statues of Jesus, sing-alongs with Black Christian choirs, sage-burning ceremonies and peace circles led by Indigenous leaders, and visitors from around the world of different classes and creeds, all of whom came to pay their respects to the temple and its land. It was a place of spirituality, not of exclusionary religious politics.

We didn't need much to be happy. In Montreal, we lived off a combination of welfare and donations from people who attended Mata's meditation center. To my surprise, Mata was able to mobilize a large community of Montrealers who would come over, especially on Sundays, for meditation and discussion. Mata was a leader, a mobilizer, people gravitated toward her. It is something that I always admired about her.

For breakfast, instead of Indian delicacies fragrant with the aroma of curry, coriander, and cumin, we ate plain oatmeal; for lunch or dinner, big plates of tofu and bowls of lentil soup. It was far from typical North American fare, but Jugy and I never complained. We were grateful for what we had and for the life we were now living, reunited with our mata.

"The more grateful you are, the more you will receive," she always said. To this day, those words ring true.

SHORTLY AFTER WE HAD BEGUN UNPACKING our belongings into the white chest of drawers that separated the single beds in our spacious room, there was a knock on the front door.

"Come on in—it's open!" Mata yelled as she walked from the kitchen to the front door. Jugy and I stuck our heads out of the bedroom doorway just far enough to see her kissing a man on the cheek. He was slightly taller than her, with brown eyes and blond hair, and wore a dark green puffer jacket, blue knit hat, and big black boots into which his pant legs had been tucked. "Ma belle, bonjour. Où sont tes gars?" ("Where are your boys?"), he asked in a deep, bellowing voice.

We looked at each other. Who was this man, and what was he doing in our home?

"Jugy? Bala? Come, someone's here to meet you." We timidly stepped into the hallway and approached the foyer where Mata and the stranger were standing. Her hand was on his back.

"This is André," she said as he stuck his hand out to shake ours. We were confused. She didn't fully explain who this man, who had apparently come to have dinner with us, was, but as the evening progressed, it became clear that he was Mata's boyfriend. Mata had prepared the most delicious homemade vegetarian lasagna, salad, and tarte au sucre—a traditional Quebec dessert. A pattern would soon be established. Every time André was around, we would have meals like this. Whenever he wasn't, it was back to the basics. I never resented Mata for this favoritism. But it did trigger some of the uneasy feelings I had when I was left behind at the ashram. On nights when we had plain meals, I would wonder why she put in more effort for André.

Although André became a fixture in our family, I never viewed him as a father figure. He didn't look like me, didn't speak like me, and, honestly, didn't seem to care to see Jugy and me as his sons. But we didn't want or expect that. I have some fond memories of him (including celebrating our first Christmas in Montreal together), but I was always aware that he wasn't my "real" father. He was just another man to me—not someone I loved, or wanted to love.

I'm more sympathetic to Mata now than I was back then. She had her own worries and challenges, and André kept her grounded. He was her sun, and her life orbited around his. If his needs, and her desire to fulfill them, took precedence over ours at times, that was okay, because she was happy. And we were together.

That first evening in Montreal, Jugy and I slept in Mata's bed. Lying between us, she stretched her arms open and we snuggled in.

My head was close enough to her chest to hear her heartbeat. Her hand wrapped around my shoulder, pulling me in closely.

"Close your eyes and listen to me," she whispered in the dark room. "I love you both, very much. I love you. I love you. I love you." She repeated the words over and over again, as if trying to convince us they were true. And we believed her. Our upbringing may not have been traditional, we may not have had family stability, but we still knew that Mata was there. We'd been miles apart, but close at heart. And now we would be together each and every day.

A WEEK AFTER JUGY AND I HAD ARRIVED, once we'd had a chance to settle in, Mata went to enroll us in school. Her top choice was an alternative arts school in our neighborhood that, despite being publicly funded, was as prestigious as the city's expensive private schools. To gain admittance, we had to apply and then be chosen by the school's selection committee. Just one week in this new city, I was being judged in ways that I never had been before.

On the day we went to visit the school, Mata made sure our hair was combed and our clothes ironed. Upon our arrival, the office staff welcomed us, before taking us to speak with the principal in his office. He sat behind a large oak desk whose color matched the brown suit he wore.

"Bonjour! Bienvenue dans notre école!" ("Welcome to our school!"), he said enthusiastically as we seated ourselves on the wide leather chairs in front of him. When Mata—who had always spoken to us in English—explained that we had yet to learn French but that she was planning to teach us as much as possible before we started school, he looked surprised. Sitting there quietly and patiently, I saw him take notes when Mata spoke. I guess he was compiling the information he needed to assess our worthiness for inclusion.

"Je parlerai avec le comité d'admission et vous contacterai la semaine prochaine" ("I'll speak with the admissions committee and contact you next week"), he said as he stood up to shake Mata's hand.

"Come on, boys," she whispered to us. "Let's go."

When we got back into the car, Mata was feeling optimistic. "It went very well! I think this may be your new school!" Jugy and I didn't say a word. We were excited to go to school but were nervous about the language barrier.

"Can't we go to an English school?" I asked. Of course, being a child and a newcomer, I had no idea about the intricacies of Quebec's educational system. We were too young to understand Bill 101, but all we knew was, despite the fact that we previously attended an English school in the US, like pawns in the Quebec education system, we were obliged to attend a French school. Languages and cultures other than French, but particularly the English language, were, with the stroke of a pen, made unwelcome in the province. Assimilation and conformity were king, and in the plainest terms, only whiteness and francophone culture would do.

The next week, Mata was asked to return and meet with the principal. This time, instead of going in with her, we waited in the car. It took only about ten minutes. As Mata walked toward us, I could tell by her the expression on her face that we were not accepted.

"Don't worry. We'll find a better school." She confidently said. I was perplexed. Jugy and I were smart. We were athletic. We were creative. We were well-mannered and kind. How could we not have been accepted? The school's decision to deny us "the best" upset me. Not because I thought I deserved it, but because I knew I did.

When we lived at the ashram, I never had a reason to see myself as "different" or "unworthy." I was confident because I was fulfilled. Because I could be myself. Because as children we were unconditionally accepted. This rejection was a rare blow to my self-esteem. And yet it would be just the first in a series of hurdles—economic, social, linguistic, racial, political, and cultural—that I would face in my life in Montreal, some of which I still need to overcome.

JUGY AND I ATTENDED OUR FIRST CLASSE D'ACCUEIL "welcome class" at École Édouard VII in Montreal's Mile End district. Built in 1912, the school's grand brownstone exterior featured a limestone-carved coat of arms above the entryway. When we stepped inside, our teacher, whose name I cannot recall, was waiting to escort us up to our classroom on the third floor. Her curly hair bounced with each step she took up the stairs as Jugy and I followed closely behind.

"C'est votre nouvelle classe" ("This is your new classroom"), she said in both languages, making sure we understood. Our classmates waved at us as we entered, and our teacher handed us each a large oatmeal cookie and a small carton of milk. We were stunned at what we took to be generosity. We didn't know that the food was part of the school's breakfast program for underprivileged immigrant children, who, they assumed, came to school on an empty stomach.

The teacher went over to two side-by-side desks at the front of the room and pulled out the chairs, gesturing for us to take a seat. They already had tags with our names on them made from white construction paper.

"Voici vos pupitres" ("Here are your desks"). Her voice was welcoming and kind. Next to us sat our new classmates: Ihab and Iham, Pablo and Pueblo, and Carlos and Marvin. We were all effectively, if not technically, immigrants. Jugy and I had been born in Canada, of course, but the country was as foreign to us as it was to our classmates. There wasn't a single francophone among us, other than our teacher. My peers looked like me, and I felt immediately at home. In fact, making friends at École Édouard VII was easy—we all accepted each other for who we were. We didn't yet know that our social cohesion was the exception, not the norm. Our classroom was a multicultural, multilingual utopia, and so we innocently assumed that the "outside world" would be just as inclusive and welcoming. It would only be a matter of time before my perfect little world got turned upside down.

Overall, the school was tolerable, but there was nothing more intolerable than the disgusting smell of meat in the cafeteria. At noon, when everyone piled onto the lunch table benches, Jugy and I would be the only kids eating packed vegetarian lunches—usually peanut butter and jelly on brown bread, an apple, some veggies, and juice. Everyone else got trays of chicken nuggets, tuna casserole, or hamburgers. It reminded us of Limestone Elementary in West Virginia.

Another thing that tripped us up was the social dynamic of the school bus. One afternoon in November, Jugy and I, unaware of the bus's social hierarchy, walked, for the first time, to the very last row, sat down, and waited for the rest of the kids to take their seats. A tall, thin boy whom I didn't recognize from my class, the lunchroom, or recess soon came up to me and started yelling at me in French.

"C'est mon siège. Bouge!" he repeated as I stared back at him in silence. I didn't understand him and I didn't know what to do. I turned to look out the window, hoping he would leave, but instead he started pushing me. It was only after I heard one of the girls from my class yell "Move!" in English that I realized I must have taken his usual seat.

"No," I replied, pushing him back. I had the right to sit where I wanted, and I refused to let a bully tell me what I could and couldn't do. To my surprise, he turned around without saying a word and walked up to the front of the bus as the rest of the students whispered to their seatmates in French. I wasn't sure what I had done; maybe my country-kid grit scared him, or the other kids, or both. Jugy looked at me and smiled.

My luck didn't last long, though. The next day at recess, the same boy approached me in the yard. It was cold and grey outside, snow flurries falling on the patchwork ski jacket Mata had brought home for me the day after we had arrived. Again, he spoke in French. Again, I answered in English.

"T'es qui, toi?" ("Who do you think you are?"), he yelled, shoving me in the chest.

"What are you doing?" I scowled, nearly losing my footing on the slippery pavement. He had crossed the line, again, and I wasn't going to back down. I sucker punched him, a right hook to the jaw. He fell hard, and after three more punches, it was over. There wasn't even enough time for people to gather around us. My aggression was as precise as it was swift.

I stood up just as the school's social worker was making his way over to us, my heart pounding from the adrenaline.

"Ça suffit! Arrête! Stop!" he yelled, but he was too late. The deed was done. Before I knew it, I was being dragged by the collar to the principal's office. I couldn't understand what was being said to me, except for two words: "Rocky Balboa." Yeah, that was me. A fighter.

That afternoon, after spending most of the day in the principal's office, I boarded the bus with the rest of my classmates. But this time, I sat in the front. The fight had nothing to do with a seat on the bus. It had to do with respect. And now, it seemed like I had that. That bully would no longer talk down to me or ask me to move. He would even try to be my friend.

As Jugy and I grew more accustomed to our new school, our new community, and our new language, we felt more included, and to our surprise, we fell in love with Montreal. In the fall, the school took us apple picking; in the winter, they taught us how to ice skate. In the spring, we visited *cabanes à sucre*, where farmers turned tree sap into delicious maple syrup. Being exposed to all things "Quebec" was something we welcomed and enjoyed.

AFTER WE WERE SETTLED, Mata began to take Jugy and me on regular trips to visit family—her brother Bob; her sister, Christiane; and Christiane's spouse and children—in a suburb outside of Montreal. On the way to meeting them for the first time, Jugy and I sat in the backseat of the car, complaining about the forty-minute drive. We didn't understand why we had to go. Mata, however, didn't give us a choice.

"You're going to meet your cousins, and you're going to have fun with them."

"But Mata, we can't even talk to them," I retorted. Learning French at school had been challenging, and I was dreading trying to carry out a basic conversation with my francophone family members. "You'll have fun, I promise," Mata said. She was always right, but despite that, I was still anxious, as Jugy and I were uncomfortable and felt somewhat shy.

"You will try French, and they will try English. Compromise." Mata's words, at the time, frustrated me. But they became one of the guiding principles of my life. Compromising. Understanding. Working together. Building bridges instead of putting up walls.

When Christiane opened the door to their large, split-level house, Mata rushed to hug her while Jugy and I crept up behind, not saying a word. In this situation, we weren't our normal outspoken, rowdy selves. We were shy and timid. When Christiane and Mata finally broke from their embrace, Christiane turned toward us, gesturing for us to come in.

"Allez, entrez," she said with a smile. We took a few steps inside as she and Mata kept talking, their banter quick and friendly. It was like walking into a foreign environment where everything was new and strange. Not only did everyone look, act, and speak differently (there was a lot of kissing and hugging that I wasn't used to, and people drank and smoked), but on full display in the living room next to the fireplace hung a taxidermied ferret, its fangs out and paws up. We were shocked. Coming from a community of vegetarians who adamantly believed that killing animals was a sin, I was frightened by and appalled at the sight of a dead animal on display. It was all so different, but my mother's family was so warm and loving, that we felt safe despite our discomfort.

"Ils sont gênés" ("They're shy"), my uncle Roland grumbled. Not just shy, Jugy and I were flustered. With her spiritual connections and unique free-spiritedness, Mata was different from her family, but she understood how to balance both worlds, the material and the spiritual. We, on the other hand, were like cubs entering a new habitat for the first time, and we needed Mata to teach us the ropes.

Mata and Christiane brought out some photo albums to show us "our roots." In them, we saw Grandpa Ernest, Uncle Bob, Mata's cousin Joanne, and so many others. It seemed like there were hundreds of pictures to flip through. But my grandma was only in a few.

"How come Grandma isn't in more of these?" I innocently asked Mata, unaware of the tension I created with my question. Mata pulled me and Jugy aside instead of addressing it at the table, where we were all sitting.

"Grandma lived a hard and difficult life. She was very sad. And one day, when I was young, she passed away," Mata explained cryptically. After leaving Christiane's home, Jugy and I still had questions, and Mata was being more open with us than she had been in the past. She described the car ride to the hospital and the circumstances leading up to our grandma's suicide. It was a lot for us to take in, especially being so young. We didn't know how to react.

"I'm sorry, Mata."

In the rearview mirror, we made eye contact. The lights of the oncoming traffic were just bright enough for me to make out her smile, and the tears that flowed from her blue eyes.

In that moment, I started to realize the pain that Mata still felt about her mother's loss. All these years later, it still brought her quickly to tears. I have since wondered if she felt like part of her soul died when her mother did, or if the stress of grappling with it alone never allowed her to make peace with it. Oddly, though, whenever we spent time with Mata's family, she seemed more upset about her mother than when we didn't. Perhaps being around them made her realize the immensity of her loss. Perhaps, too, it brought back memories of when they had been a family—memories that gave her comfort but that also highlighted the gaping hole in the family since her mother's death. It was complicated, unresolved, and wearying.

MATA DIDN'T TALK MUCH about our father. And while, in truth, we didn't think about him much during the initial months after our arrival, we did know he lived in Montreal. Over time, as our curiosity about his whereabouts increased, so did the pressure we put on Mata to see him.

Whenever we brought it up, she would nod but wouldn't promise to arrange a meeting. It wasn't until midsummer, nearly five months after we had arrived in Canada, that we were finally reunited. To this day, I'm not sure why Mata kept us apart for so long. Pita wasn't the type to call, and Mata clearly didn't seem concerned about our relationship with our father; at least, she made no obvious effort to reach out to him.

"Pita is coming today," Mata told us as we ate breakfast one hot July morning. The humidity was nearly unbearable, the air thick and heavy. Jugy and I were shocked. Mata hadn't mentioned speaking to Pita, let alone inviting him over to see us. Suddenly, I was eager to see him.

"Today?" I asked, my voice raising with excitement.

"Yes, any minute now," Mata replied, just as we heard a knock on the front door. Peering down the hallway from the kitchen at the back of the apartment, I could see Pita through the door's glass. Backlit by the sun, his body cast a shadow into the foyer. I could feel his aura. Strong. Confident. Distinguished.

Mata opened the door. "Bala? Jugy?" As Pita's deep voice echoed through the apartment, we got up from the table and ran to him without any hesitation. Though we had seen him only once in nine years, and hardly knew anything about him, our connection was immediate and undeniable.

Kneeling down, he opened his arms wide, welcoming us into his embrace. He smelled of sandalwood and the sweet mangoes he had brought with him. Without saying much, we walked back to the kitchen, Mata leading the way. Instead of sitting down with us at the table, Pita went straight to the sink to wash and peel the fruit while Mata took a plate out of the cupboard. The slices of sweet, delicious mango he presented to us smelled—and tasted— like candy.

I am unsure why I immediately accepted Pita without judgment— why, after he had stayed away for most of our short lives, I felt no anger toward him. Now that he was here, all I wanted was to sit with him, listen to his stories, and tell him that I loved him. I suppose his absence hadn't hurt me because I had no expectations for our relationship. Or maybe it was because I was so supported, fulfilled, and empowered by the community at the ashram and by my spirituality, I felt no void in my heart for him. I was enlightened enough to accept and forgive his absence.

Pita won my and Jugy's hearts with his fatherly energy and through the genuine interest he seemed to take in us—and the time he began to spend with us. I remember him arriving unannounced at our home one morning. As Mata walked toward the door she yelled back, "Did you invite someone here?" But Jugy and I hadn't. We were just as curious and confused as she. As soon as Mata unlocked the door, we heard Pita's deep voice rumble and then, without hesitation, crescendo until we could hear him clearly.

"Bala? Jugy? Come on! We're going on an adventure!" To our surprise, Pita had gotten us tickets to see the Montreal Expos. I had never seen a live baseball game before, so when we heard his plans, Jugy and I were ecstatic.

We took the metro to Pie-IX station, just outside Montreal's infamous Olympic stadium (built for the 1976 Summer Olympics in Montreal)—the same metro station where, years prior, Pita and Mata had gone to on their way to the Hindu temple. The stadium's grandeur was unlike anything I had experienced before. Our seats, made from hard plastic, were in one of the balcony sections. The artificial grass field looked like it went on for miles and miles. It reminded me of the fields in West Virginia where Jugy and I had played with our friends. The experience was new and exciting for us. As the players ran onto the field, the announcer's voice boomed over the stadium speakers, asking everyone to remove their caps and stand for the national anthem.

The collective singing and patriotism was something I hadn't seen on such a large scale before. The voices of the nearly twenty thousand people at the game were like a choir, led by their love of the sport, the team, and the country. As the game began, we watched intently, the crowd cheering each time a batter made it onto first base or rounded in for a run. But as minutes turned to hours, our excitement began to fade. Watching professional baseball, we came to realize, required a lot of patience—more than either Jugy or I had.

Just as my attention began to drift away from the game and onto the crowd, there was a sharp cracking sound. Henry Rodriguez had hit a fastball into the seats for a home run! The whole stadium erupted, Jugy and I jumping up from our seats to join in. To our surprise, amidst the cheering and the blaring music, fans started throwing Oh Henry! chocolate bars onto the field. Apparently, this was a tradition every time Rodriguez hit a home run.

"Oh Henry! Oh Henry! Oh Henry!" they chanted as he rounded third base, arms raised above his head as he pumped his fists into the air. My excitement about the run, though, was quickly replaced by confusion. Turning to Jugy, I yelled, "I can't believe someone would throw away a chocolate bar like that!"

"I know!" he answered back, equally astonished. Pita started to laugh when he overheard our conversation. Since we had grown up poor, it was inconceivable to us that someone would buy a chocolate bar just to throw it away.

As the game finished and people started pouring out of the stadium, we stayed in our seats, letting the rest of the game-goers in our row scoot past us on their way toward the exit. When nearly everyone in our section had left, Pita got up and grabbed our hands. We followed him out, down the grey concrete steps sticky from old gum and spilled soda.

"One second, come here," Pita whispered before making a left turn and leading us down a narrow corridor whose walls were painted with the Expos logo. In front of us was a refreshment stand, the last one open in the stadium.

"Two Oh Henrys!, please."

..

THOUGH BASEBALL ALWAYS HELD a special place in my and Jugy's hearts after that day, it required a patience that didn't come naturally to us. And so to satisfy our love of action and speed we turned to hockey—a sport deeply ingrained in Quebec culture. A sport that united the city, especially when, on June 9, 1993, the Montreal Canadiens won the Stanley Cup. We didn't have cable, but the antenna we fashioned out of a coat hanger wrapped in tinfoil gave us just enough channels to watch the game and the news. The Habs's victory against Wayne Gretzky and the Los Angeles Kings, taking place more than seventy-five years after their first Stanley Cup win, set the city ablaze, quite literally—at certain points, the celebrations, which lasted for days, gave way to rioting. Joining in the hype, Jugy and I played street hockey in the alley behind our house. Whether together or with our friends, this became our main summer pastime. As summer turned into fall and we became better at stick-handling and scoring, we asked Mata if we could join a "real" team.

We didn't have pads, but after a bit of convincing, Mata bought us some used equipment. It was well-worn but served its purpose. The day Jugy first put on his black helmet, and I my red one, we knew that our hobby was about to turn into an organized, competitive sport. And sure enough, we soon began playing in Rosemont's Atom B League. The team was diverse and included some of our classmates from École Édouard VII, but we all spoke French instead of English. Many of the players had parents or siblings who had also, at some point, been on the team. Hockey, we came to realize, was a legacy sport, a community pastime that defined families for generations.

Jugy and I both played forward—we could barely skate, but we were scrappy and we could whack at the puck harder than most kids. During our first game of the season, I clearly remember my wobbly skating, the puck ricocheting off my helmet as I fell next to the goalie. Without realizing that I had just (involuntarily) scored a goal, I got up and meandered back to the bench, avoiding eye contact with my teammates and coaches, embarrassed at what I had assumed was a poor play. I knew my skates weren't as sharp as the other kids', but I held myself to such a high standard that I was flustered about the fall. As I approached the bench, however, my coach began clapping. Booming over the arena's speakers, I heard the announcer read out my name.

"But! [Goal!] Bal-ah-rah-mah Holness!" I couldn't believe it. I had done what I set out to do. I was making a difference. I was helping my team.

I had always excelled at sports. It was part of my DNA. But scoring a goal in my first organized hockey game was something that made me especially proud. After the game, Jugy and I waited outside the rink for Mata to pick us up. As our teammates piled out of the building, they high-fived us on the way to their parents' cars.

"Where's Mata?" I asked Jugy after nearly twenty minutes of waiting.

"Maybe she forgot," Jugy replied, standing up from the concrete stairs where we had been sitting. It was getting dark, the once bright blue sky settling into a deep navy.

"Let's just take the bus home," he said, picking up his hockey bag and gesturing for me to do the same. The walk to the bus was only twenty minutes, but for ten-year-olds carrying forty-pound bags, it felt like a cross-country trek. I was sweaty, despite the cool spring weather. I was hot. I was disappointed.

When we got home, Mata's car was parked outside in its usual spot. She must have been busy, or lost track of time. When we walked inside, Jugy greeted her and ran to the dinner table. I quietly said hello, trying to avoid conversation. Mata's "lapses" were a trigger for me; her failure to pick us up was a painful reminder of her many absences over the past nine years. In my mind, if Mata really loved me, she wouldn't have left me at the arena. As an adult, I can see that my reaction wasn't fair. Jugy was wiser. He always understood that Mata did what she had to do to give us the best life she could. She was a hustler. She was ambitious. She worked *for us*. But I held her to such a high standard that anything that deviated from my ideal perception of a "mother" was difficult to accept.

MATA'S WORK ETHIC WAS INDEFATIGABLE; she did everything in her power to keep the fridge full and Jugy and me engaged in school and extracurriculars. Along with hockey, she enrolled us in swimming at the YMCA and football with the Sun Youth Hornets Football Club. I distinctly remember Mata taking us to the field, the coach passing out pads and balls for our first practice. Jugy and I loved football. Within minutes of being on the field, we were throwing the ball and tackling each other. The sport reminded us of the rough and rowdy games we played with our friends at the ashram. But Mata wasn't a fan.

"No more football. It's too rough. You're going to get hurt," she told us as soon as practice had ended. We protested, but Mata's mind was already made up. The next day, she pulled us out of the club. Little did she, or I, know that I would be playing professional football for my hometown team just fifteen years after that practice.

I attribute much of my life's success to the sports I played as a young adult, but also as a child. Athleticism came naturally to me. Sports were fulfilling. They were a tool that I used to learn, not just about myself, but about others, and about my new city. They helped me make connections and gain respect. Hockey, rather than school, taught me how to speak French and made me and Jugy feel comfortable living in Montreal. Simply put, sports saved me.

We even got to play in school, not just at recess but in intramural leagues with our classmates. Sports infiltrated every aspect of our lives. And we wouldn't have had it any other way.

ONCE WE REUNITED WITH PITA, Mata would drop us off at his apartment in social housing on the weekends. About a forty-minute bus ride from ours, it was tucked behind a park in West-mount, adjacent to some noisy train tracks. I was too young to fully understand his situation, but I later came to realize that Pita, like Mata, lived on welfare. His experiences in the workforce had not been successful. He had personal challenges as well as a general dejectedness—he simply did not want to work in science, or for anyone, for that matter. His motivations in life were spiritual and intellectual. He was also unable to integrate into Quebec society. Connected to God but disconnected from his community, he be-came increasingly jaded and recognized himself as an outcast who "did not fit in anywhere he went." His social exclusion took a fur-ther toll on his mental health as his marginality became his new re-ality. Once an active member of his community in Jamaica, he was now socially and economically excluded from his Canadian home.

Pita's humble abode was like a disorganized museum filled with books, clothes, vintage cologne, training weights, musical instru-ments, tech gadgets, sports memorabilia, paintings, African masks, and jewelry collected from garage sales across Montreal. For Jugy and me, Pita's house was a jungle where we would partake in wild treasure hunts every time we visited.

Pita's massive library introduced Jugy and me to a whole new world: Aristotle, Michel Foucault, and Taoism and other religious tenets. He would lecture us about the world, telling us what it would take to be "superior men." At the time, I didn't completely understand what he meant; I just knew that books, knowledge, and listening would be part of my path to becoming "superior"—or, at the very least, empowered. Perhaps Pita told us this because, being seen by others as a poor Black immigrant, he lived in the proverbial basement of society. For Jugy and me, however, he had the radiant magnetism of a king: I can only describe his presence and aura as otherworldly.

One of my favorite memories of Pita was when he, sporting thigh-high cotton shorts, taught us how to "dance through life." With the sunlight beaming through his window, he glossed aloe and ghee all over his body.

"This is how it's done, boys," he said proudly in his thick Jamaican accent. He placed large crystals at the base of water-filled glass jars that sat on the edge of the window, creating mini-rainbows throughout the room. He put on some upbeat reggae music, grabbed two ten-pound weights, and began to dance. With his five-foot-long dreadlocks swinging like the blades of a helicopter, he swerved and grooved to the music with his eyes closed, as if in a trance. As the room heated up and his body glowed with sweat, he opened his eyes and said, "effortless effort," before shutting them and continuing to dance. Jugy and I watched in awe. Pita looked like a transcendental, free man. That mantra, "effortless effort," was one my father applied to everything, from sports to politics and everything in-between. It summed up his feelings about how life should be lived and work performed.

After taking a cold shower, Pita sat me and Jugy down around a pile of books and old newspapers. As we read them, I kept coming across words and names that I'd never seen before.

"Who is Noam Chomsky?" I asked.

"You don't know who Chomsky is?" Pita said. He appeared shocked, as if every twelve-year-old should know who the American linguist and philosopher was. From hegemony to imperialism, that afternoon Pita taught me Chomsky's take on US foreign policy. I came away with an understanding of the basics: that the United States, through the power of its military, was able to control other countries.

But that early lesson would have a profound impact on me. Throughout my life, I've continued to follow Chomsky, particularly his writings on US foreign policy and imperialism. Among other things, the countless conversations Pita and I had about these topics over the years made me question the role and power of activism as an agent of change. Am I going to be arguing about poverty, health inequalities, and racial profiling fruitlessly until the end of my days, just like Chomsky has about US imperialism? Or will the world change for the better? From systemic racism to US imperialism, I genuinely ask myself if alternatives are possible. As far as Pita was concerned, the world was perfect—it did not need fixing. We were all just experiencing our own karma in the material word.

Although Pita never said "I love you" to me and Jugy, he showed his love through his actions. Little things, like cooking a warm meal, made us feel—and taste—his affection. It was one of the ways we understood that we were being cared for. With ghee, vegetables, spices, dough, and a cast-iron wok, he could create just about any Indian dish for us, samosas being our favorite. I can still smell meals he put in front of us: a base of pita bread stacked with samosas, French fries, avocado, and homegrown sprouts. Though we'd grown up away from our father, the simple pleasures of time, attention, and a warm meal were enough to build our bond.

His absence from our lives was something he feverishly defended time and time again. "Your mother kidnapped you from me," he would say to us as Jugy sat on an empty bucket and I on a small stool in his tiny kitchen. It was hard to take a bite of food without knocking something over. Maybe he didn't consent to Mata taking us away, but we never really believed that we were "kidnapped." Had he chased after us like I used to chase Mata when she left in the early mornings, I would have believed him. But, he didn't. He was stagnant, just like Mata had thought years before. Later, I learned from Mata that he remarried and had two more kids. I had no knowledge of or connection with his new family. What I did know is that he was not with his wife, nor was he taking care of his other kids. Despite all his flaws, I never judged him. I was just happy that we were reunited.

Whenever we got ready to leave Pita's house, Jugy and I felt sad. Deep down, I had a sense of loss about not having been around my father when I was growing up. Every time we left, I wondered if I would ever see him again, even though we lived just a few miles away. I also looked up to him and admired how he lived, in complete control over his schedule and actions. In reality, though, that "freedom" came at a cost: loneliness and isolation. Although his books and gadgets provided Jugy and me with entertainment and education, for Pita, they must have felt like a trap sometimes.

"Do you get lonely, Pita?" I asked him each time before we left. He always responded with the same assurance: "God is my best friend. With him, I don't get lonely." I was never fully convinced of this, though. Jugy and I knew that we, his true companions, provided the jolt of energy and family that he must have craved. His innumerable material possessions didn't change the fact that without us, without family, he really had nothing.

ON THE LAST DAY of our first full year of school in Montreal, before the summer holidays, Mata came to pick us up so that she could talk to our teacher and principal about how our school year had gone. We didn't expect much of the meeting, except maybe for them to talk about our grades or the comments our teacher had made about our being "rowdy" in class. We waited in the hallway as they chatted, the minutes feeling like hours.

"Jugy? Bala?" we heard Mata say as the door to the classroom opened. "Come here, we have some questions to ask you." Jugy and I walked inside and sat down at the desks nearest to the door. By now, we could sense that something was wrong, but we weren't sure what.

"Next year, do you want to stay in grade five or move onto grade six?" Mata asked. I was confused. Our French was still limited, but we had passed our grade five classes.

"Why would we redo a grade we were just in?" I asked.

"Your teacher thinks that you could use the French practice. It might give you more time to learn—to feel more comfortable." I still didn't understand. I could speak a decent amount of French. I didn't know what to say.

"I don't know," I repeated, looking at Mata. Her usual radiant smile was gone. She looked concerned. Perhaps she didn't know what to do either. After a long pause, Mata turned toward us and then back to our teacher and the principal.

"Keep them in grade five. It can't hurt."

I sat in silence. The ramifications of the decision Mata had just made for me and Jugy weren't yet clear, but over the next few weeks I came to realize that with those five words Mata was going to take me away from my friends. Take me away from the people I was used to. It made me feel like I wasn't good enough, or smart enough, to "do" school the way that all the other kids did. It was the first time I felt inferior, not superior, like Pita kept preaching.

"It's okay, Bala. We'll be together, just like we were last year," Jugy said to me whenever I brought it up. And he was right. Jugy and I would get through it together, just like we did everything. Time and time again, Jugy was my rock.

But it turned out Mata was right. Grade five wasn't so bad the second time around. We were adaptable and made new friends quickly. Our French was also rapidly improving. Each day after school, we would get off the bus, walk from the intersection to the *ruelle* behind our home, and open up the side door that led into the kitchen. Mata would usually be standing behind the counter, making us an after-school snack to eat before we started our homework or went outside to play with our friends.

One afternoon in mid-June, a week before the end of the school year, things were different. When we stepped inside, we saw Mata pacing up and down the hallway, searching the house as if she'd lost something important.

"Mata? What's going on?" I said.

"Jugy, get Bala and come to the dinner table," Mata said. She was clearly flustered, having mistakenly called me Jugy.

"Jugy, come here!" I yelled. Jugy had already gone to our bedroom to start his homework. Without saying a word, he joined us. He was the smarter and more studious of the two of us. He talked less than me. He listened more. He was more patient and less impulsive. In that way, he was just like Pita. Mata sat down, exhaled loudly, and took our hands.

"We've lived here for nearly two years. I like it, and I know you both do too. But I've been missing my family, especially my cousin Joanne, who you haven't yet met. She was one of my best friends growing up. I really love her, and being apart from her is difficult for me." Mata paused. Before continuing, she looked at both of us, checking for our reaction. But our expressions didn't give anything away.

"What do you think about moving to her town? It's called Boisbriand." I looked at Jugy, my eyes growing wide in shock, hoping that he had an answer for Mata. Jugy always knew what to say and do. When we played chess, he moved his pieces in the most perfect formations, beating me every time. I hoped that his prowess on the board would translate to nuance in this conversation because, as it stood, it didn't seem like we had a choice in the matter.

"We don't want to leave, Mata. We just got here. Pita is here. And we just made friends again," replied Jugy. Mata was disappointed, especially after I echoed Jugy's stance. To me it was clear—we would be leaving Pita just at the point when we had started to rebuild our relationship. Mata would be taking us away from him, again. Was this because of what she'd said about him a few days earlier, that he was "lazy"? I didn't know how to communicate what was going on inside of my head, but I was not happy.

"You'll make new friends, and your cousin Richard will be there too. You can still play hockey, and maybe even soccer. You'll have fun." With those words, everything we had built, all the friendships we had made, vanished before our eyes. Mata always told us that we would have fun. She was usually right, but we were skeptical. At any rate, it seemed like there was nothing we could do to get out of it.

As Mata continued talking about the move, I noticed the suitcase we had used just two years earlier to move from West Virginia to Montreal leaning against the back wall of the foyer. A purple shirt sleeve was sticking out of the zipper and a few pairs of socks were sitting on its top.

Once again, we were about to leave everything behind. Unlike the "independent" choices she made to travel when we lived at the ashram, however, Mata's decision to leave affected our lives, changed our plans, and reoriented our path. It seemed to come out of the blue. And, unbeknownst to me, Jugy, or Mata herself, this time it would really change our lives forever.

FOUR

DOMINATION BY ASSIMILATION

I remember it distinctly—the rush, the uncertainty, the unknown. I was glued to Jugy, head resting on him like a pillow, as the muffler of Mata's Toyota sputtered down Grand Allée, the main road of Boisbriand, a middle-class suburb of twenty-five thousand just out-side Montreal. André followed behind us in a small moving truck filled with furniture and our precious hockey gear—everything we needed to get set up in our new town.

"On est arrivés" ("We've arrived"), Mata said gently to Jugy and me as she parked behind the three-story grey brick building that housed our new apartment. We sat in the backseat, in no rush to get out of the car. Tired and unenthusiastic about yet another "adventure," as Mata called it, we didn't say much to her or to each other. I felt like a bird that was always flying from place to place, building and rebuilding nests with each flight. But I didn't feel empowered; I felt like I was losing my feathers.

After climbing out of the driver's seat, Mata smiled at us through the backseat window. "Let's go," she said, opening the door and gesturing for us to jump out. "Get your bags out of the trunk. André will bring the rest up while we go get some groceries." Jugy and I weren't thrilled about the fact that André was moving in with us full time and that we were now even farther away from Pita.

Her smile was comforting, her aura reassuring, but I still had my doubts. Though at heart I was a wild and scrappy country kid who loved adventures, I also longed for the stability of home, and, most of all, of family. We had left Pita and our newly forming relationship with him behind in Montreal, and André was definitely not a father figure to me. For one thing, we clashed culturally. His French nationalism was clear, and honestly, I felt like he took advantage of Mata's kindness and generosity. Without contributing much to our family, he still acted like we "owed" him respect. Even when I was young, I knew that respect had to be earned. And it wouldn't be easy for André to get it from me. I still had Jugy and Mata, though, so I hoped everything would be okay.

The supermarket was just a few blocks away, down the hill from our spacious two-bedroom apartment. As we walked toward the store's grand entrance, its automatic door slid open and a gush of cold air-conditioning came rushing out.

"Bonjour," Mata said to a staff member sitting near the front of the store.

"Hi," we said in English. He smiled gently as we walked by him on our way to the produce section. As we headed down each aisle, I couldn't help but notice a homogeneity I wasn't used to—not of the food, but of the people. Jugy and I were the only people in the store with dark skin and curly hair. This was new for us. We were used to diverse, multicultural Montreal and New Vrindaban, where our multifaceted identity was reflected in everyday life. But here, within minutes of arriving, it was clear that we had entered a completely new universe.

"Why are you staring?" Mata whispered to me in English, a

language only a minority of Boisbriand residents spoke. I didn't know how to answer. I was experiencing culture shock yet again. I turned to Jugy, but his eyes were glued to the candy aisle.

"I'm not staring, I'm just looking," I said, but I could tell Mata wasn't satisfied with my answer. Honestly, I don't think she liked our attitude to the move in general. We knew we would miss our friends, and not just because we'd grown close to them, but because they were part of a community that we felt at home in and that accepted us for who we were.

MATA HAD ARRANGED FOR US TO ATTEND a French primary school, which was also down the hill and across the park from our new apartment. Compared to our bus rides in Montreal, and our uphill trek at the ashram, this was an easy walk. We were still on welfare, and Mata was selling classical music CDs door to door to make ends meet.

When Mata dropped us off at our new school, Jugy and I were impressed. Unlike Édouard VII, everything here was new and shiny—even the bricks sparkled. The administrators and teachers seemed nice, but, to our disappointment, Jugy and I were separated into different grade six classes. Since kindergarten, we had always been together. It was how we learned best, how we felt most comfortable. But we didn't have a choice. Choice—or the lack of it—played a big role in my time in Boisbriand. Not only was the choice to move made for us, so were the decisions about our education, what language we were allowed to speak, and, as I would soon discover, what I would be called.

On the first day of class I took my assigned seat in the middle of the classroom. The teacher, Mr. Lepage, began taking attendance. It was a ritual I had grown accustomed to at Édouard VII, so, not thinking much of it, I waited for my name to be called.

"Ba—la—ra—ma? Hullness?" Mr. Lepage said, scanning the classroom before locking eyes with me: the brown kid with curly hair who stuck out like a sore thumb.

"Oui, présent," I mumbled, raising my hand halfway. I could hear a few students whisper and laugh. I wasn't entirely sure why I was being ridiculed, but I felt ashamed nonetheless and shrank in my seat. Not knowing what to say, I put my hand down and waited for my teacher to finish roll call. I thought he would welcome me, or ask the class to say hello, but I got nothing. He simply looked down at the class list and continued calling out names.

"Antoine Lemieux?" Check. "Marie Gagnon?" Check. "Emmanuelle Dugas?" Check. I could hear the kids in the class whispering "Quoi?" "Quoi?" "Quoi?"—"What?" "What?" "What?"

Once class was over, Mr. Lepage calmly approached me.

"Ba-lara-ma? Do you go by another name? Is there something else I can call you?" To my surprise, he spoke to me in English. I guess I didn't realize how obvious it was that I wasn't comfortable with French. Or maybe he just assumed that, because of my skin color, I wasn't "French."

"No, Balarama's my name. But my friends call me Bala," I responded.

"Bala?" he questioned, again sounding confused. I didn't understand what was wrong, but I felt demoralized.

Walking home that day, I told Jugy how much I hated being in Boisbriand. "We just got here, and I already can't stand it."

"Me too!" Jugy said, briefly putting his hand on my shoulder. "After class was over, the teacher called me Jonathan instead of Jagannatha."

"I told my teacher to call me Bala, and he looked at me weirdly," I answered back.

When we arrived home, Mata was waiting for us in the kitchen.

"Salut!" she called as the front door creaked open.

"Mata!" we yelled, kicking off our shoes and running to tell her about our awful day.

But instead of telling me that I should be proud of my name, as I expected, Mata dismissed my concerns, waving them away. I was stunned by her response. It felt as though she knew that this would happen. I knew deep down that she cared about who I was and how I felt in this new town, but in that moment, she didn't seem to. Jugy didn't even bother telling her about the whole "Jonathan" thing. She was certainly aware that Jugy and I would have to adapt to the environment, to the people and culture, but she didn't prepare us for these challenges. We felt stuck.

By the end of my first month of school, my teacher suggested random names, Dominic, Françis, Steven, and so on, instead of Balarama. It was also odd because Mata went along with it. Steven it was. Although it was supposed to seem like a recommendation, the subtext was that it would be necessary for me to assimilate into the larger group. But I knew that was wrong. I felt violated. Castrated. Crucified. All at the same time. In the name of social cohesion, it was as if society was trying to generate a profile for me rather than letting me be myself.

"I'm Bala, though. Why do you need to call me something else?" But in this new place I felt alone, shy, and submissive, like a young lion that had lost its roar.

Who I was—my name and identity—was simply not accepted by my teacher, my classmates, or anyone I had interacted with in Boisbriand in the short time that we had lived there. Everyone thought that something was off about me. I was too different. I felt like a fish out of water.

Looking back, I wish I had stood up for myself. Years later, I would have dreams in which I told my teacher, "I'm Balarama!

That's my name. Learn it and pronounce it right!" But I was impressionable and wanted to easily assimilate. And so from that day on, when he called attendance, Mr. Lepage referred to me as "Steven." And I would raise my hand. Over time, I got used to it. If a stranger asked me what my name was, I would say "Steven." If a friend or family addressed me, though, it was always "Bala."

I didn't realize it then, but I was having an identity crisis at the age of eleven. When I first arrived in Canada, assimilation seemed pleasant: learning French, taking outings to sugar cabins and apple farms, playing and watching ice hockey, and seeing free French movies at the theater. Now, in this middle-class French suburb, I felt like I was being tamed. I had grown up without parents, rarely feeling loved. If being tamed meant receiving acceptance and love from people around me, well then, I would be tamed.

IT WASN'T LONG BEFORE JUGY AND I discovered that the kids at school were divided into two groups: the "YOs" (kids who wore baggy clothes and liked hip-hop) and the "Skaters" (those who listened to alternative and rock music and wore chunky, padded skate shoes). I'm not sure if it was my skin color, my first language, or because I wore the same clothes over and over again, but I was boxed in with the YOs.

One day, a group of older skaters from high school intercepted me and Jugy on the way home from school. They made us wait with our backs to a fence and questioned us about who we were and why we were part of the YOs. We weren't sure ourselves—we were just spiritually minded kids from an ashram. Why had we been identified and categorized? We couldn't answer their question.

Society has an odd way of forcing people into groups without their consent, using manufactured labels that often are incorrect, unjust, and nonsensical. Because Jugy and I had grown up on the ashram, where such things didn't happen, Boisbriand's labeling system felt as foreign to us as we were to it. We were too atypical to fit into any group, and yet we were still compartmentalized in both the schoolyard and the educational system. But assimilation also had a major benefit, namely, social acceptance and integration.

We started hanging out on weekends with one of our classmates, Marc-André. We mostly played at his house, where we spent hours mastering Tekken on his PlayStation gaming console. One afternoon, Marc-André's mother, Julie, asked if I wanted to stay for dinner. I had been such an outcast that I welcomed this bit of warmth. So I accepted, but, embarrassed to be a bother, I didn't tell Julie that I was a vegetarian. I knew it would mean more work for her, and honestly, it was something I didn't want to share. I just wanted to fit in.

I immediately became anxious when she called us upstairs for dinner. I had smelled the aroma of cooking meat for the previous half hour but couldn't muster the courage to say anything about it. As I sat down at the table, Julie's arm reached over my shoulder to place a big blue bowl filled with pasta and meat sauce in front of me. Being raised vegetarian, I couldn't eat meat, not just because of ethics or morals, but because of the disgust I felt thinking about (and seeing) dead animal flesh on my plate.

"Je suis végétarien" ("I'm vegetarian"), I said, timidly, trying my best to be polite. Julie looked at me confused, as if I had insulted her cooking.

"Tu es végétarien?" ("You're vegetarian?").

"Oui, je ne mange pas de viande" ("Yes, I don't eat meat"), I started to reply, but was cut off by Marc-André's father, Pierre.

"What do you eat then, just plants?" he interrupted, laughing and scoffing at my honesty.

"I guess you'll have to eat the side salad then, Steven," Julie chuck-led, confirming and reinforcing my social marginality yet again.

BEING DIFFERENT, I WOULD LEARN AS AN ADULT, was supposed to be empowering, but as a child I had no one to reassure me that my differences were my strengths, so self-doubt set in. There was an African boy in my class named Victor. He was French and seemed to fit in perfectly as one of "them"—the francophone Quebecers who made up an overwhelming majority of my classmates. It seemed I was worse off because, despite two years of French schooling, I still hadn't mastered the language. I felt like an intruder and an imposter. Even teachers and administrators chastised me and Jugy when we spoke English in the hallways. "On parle français ici!" ("We speak French here!"), they would say.

My school experience was a microcosm of the linguistic and political situation in the province as a whole. The mid-1990s were a tumultuous political time in Quebec. The province was on the cusp of holding yet another referendum on whether to separate from the rest of Canada. Where in the previous referendum so-called *pure-laine* ("pure wool") Quebecers—those descended from settlers who started coming to New France in the seventeenth century—saw the English establishment as the main threat to their language and culture, that perceived threat had now expanded to include newcomers like myself.

Unbeknownst to me, being an anglophone was a political act. Speaking English with Jugy in the school hallways, even saying something as simple as "Hi" instead of "Bonjour" to the cashier at the grocery store, was political. Even over two decades later, in 2018, the National Assembly of Quebec would put forward a motion to oblige store clerks to greet people by saying "Bonjour" rather than the colloquial, commonly used "Bonjour-Hi." That's how petty, yet political, language was—and still is—in Quebec.

Kids at school would ask me, "Do you want Quebec to separate?," but I had no clue what they were talking about. And to be honest, I don't think they knew either. Like most kids, I was too young to understand the complexity of the province's linguistic tensions, and especially how those tensions played out in my community. Everything I understood about the referendum I learned from my friends in the schoolyard. I figured I was on the "no" side of the debate since all my French classmates were pro-separation on the "oui" side. As an anglophone "immigrant," pledging allegiance to Canada made more sense than pledging allegiance to Quebec—a place that labeled me and my brother as outcasts or too different to fit in. I still didn't understand the nuances of the separation debate. From my point of view as a child, it felt like Quebec, the place I called home, didn't want me there. Separating would simply give this "nation," as the province often referred to itself, more powers to discriminate against members of minority communities, like myself. Looking back now, I see sovereignty as an aim that was meant to preserve a weakening French culture and a deteriorating moral fabric that saw people who were different as a threat. This growing concern did not inspire me to integrate into my new society; it made me want to rebel against it.

That October, in 1995, Quebecers went to the polls to vote on the future of the province. As with the 1980 referendum, the "no" camp prevailed with a narrow 50.58 percent majority; voters chose for the province to remain a part of Canada. After the referendum, there was considerable upheaval and controversy. When Premier Jacques Parizeau, who had rallied the "oui" vote as leader of the pro-separatist Parti Québécois, blamed the defeat on "money and the ethnic vote," it was a clear message of disdain toward Quebecers like me, who were anything other than white and French.

BY THE END OF THE SCHOOL YEAR, I had built up a lot of frustration. I felt like this group of people who viewed me as an outsider was trying to tame and control me. One person had even called me a "savage." So I began to rebel. I got into trouble. I fought.

My anger, though, didn't serve me well. In fact, it made my situation worse. After the teacher briefly stepped out of the classroom one day, things got wild, and a boy by the name of François called me a n———. I replied with a sucker punch that got me suspended. I hadn't even known I was Black, let alone a n———, until I came to Boisbriand. Before that I was just me.

A couple of weeks after the last day of school, I was on my way to Marc-André's house when I walked past a young boy who was playing in his yard. He looked at me, paused, and said, "T'as de la boue sur la face" ("You have mud on your face"). The boy was about three or four years old, and I was probably the first person of color he had ever seen. Without breaking stride, I looked ahead and kept walking. His words were forever etched in my brain, but I wasn't hurt. I was becoming numb to the racism, conscious or unconscious, that seemed to be an ingrained norm in Quebec society. Even young children signaled to me that I was "other"—an inferior "minority" with a skin tone that reminded them of mud. If Boisbriand was a clean white tuxedo, my presence, in the eyes of others at least, was staining it.

A few weeks later, a similar situation unfolded. I was heading home in the late afternoon when I noticed a family of four walking down the sidewalk about fifty yards in front of me. As we got closer together, I started to doubt myself, my own identity, and my presence in this white community. I was unsure whether my presence would "sully" their experience and make them uneasy, so I crossed the street to avoid them.

As I passed the family from across the street, I heard one of the children asking why I had crossed the street. The other responded, "Parce qu'il est laid" ("Because he's ugly"), and the whole family laughed. The daily experiences of living as an outsider weathered my self-confidence and shook my sense of self. I no longer moved freely in my skin. The months of being treated as different, the odd boy out by people in Boisbriand had given me an inferiority complex. Years later, it occurred to me that this was the warning Pita had been trying to give me with his "superior man" lesson.

In September 1996, Jugy and I entered seventh grade, which is the start of high school in Quebec. This involved, of course, switching schools. The first few weeks were smooth. We joined the basketball team and started to get used to our new surroundings. But whether it was our culture, our language, or the fact that we were new, or perhaps just too different, we soon began to have issues with a group of students. Rule number one with us twins is that if you have an issue with one of us, you have an issue with both of us. And so as tension increased, and dialogue decreased, Jugy and I started to solve our differences with our fists.

One morning in early December, one of my classmates threw a ball of paper at my head. I let it slide, but I knew I needed to address it.

At lunchtime, I approached the kid to ask him why he had thrown the paper at me. He said that he had issues with Jugy but didn't give details, not that I cared to know what they were. Beef with my brother put an immediate end to any conversation. So I got in the kid's face, and he pushed me. I knew from my experiences scrapping in cornfields in West Virginia that the key to winning a fight was to punch first and ask questions later, and so I did. After a few solid blows and a tackle to the ground, the fight was over in a flash, before any school administrator arrived.

As I walked away, I felt my right hand begin to swell. By the time I got back to class it had ballooned to the size of a base-ball. When I got home, I told Mata what had happened. She was surprised and disappointed but knew what Jugy and I were going through at school. A visit to the hospital and some X-rays revealed a broken hand; I would be in a cast for six weeks. Until now, my fights hadn't come with many consequences (if any at all). This time was different. A broken fist meant not playing basketball for the rest of the season. On top of that, I had an in-school suspension for a full week with different break and lunch hours than the rest of the school. I would be in the company of all kinds of bad kids, including the boy I had fought. Apart from some bruising on his face, he hadn't suffered much physical damage. But his body language told another story. Visibly dejected, he kept his head down, eyes off me, and body slouched. If I wasn't going to make a ton of friends in this new school, then at least I would gain the respect that comes from not backing down from a fight. I learned early on that it's better to be respected than to be liked.

Despite my conflict and challenges, I started to settle in and make friends. Mata had transitioned from selling CDs to selling health-care products for a multilevel marketing company and was having great success with André as a business partner. I let myself imagine what it would be like to live in Boisbriand for good. Even though I was always fighting, I was sick of feeling like we never had a stable home. My life sometimes reminded me of the heist movies Jugy and I watched on weekends: we were like those characters with ski masks, who were always on the run from someone—or *something*. I just wanted to stay in one place. Which *is* when Mata decided to move us from Boisbriand to Ottawa.

Boisbriand had its flaws, but Jugy and I still feverishly rejected this latest "escape," especially since it meant we would be even farther away from Pita, whom we already rarely saw. Though we were becoming used to making new friends and starting at new schools, ripping us away from our father was the norm but nonetheless painful. We both pleaded with Mata to stay, but her mind was made up. This time, we weren't just moving to a new city, but to a whole new province.

IN BOISBRIAND, MY BROKEN FRENCH had been a liability. In bilingual Ottawa, the nation's capital, it was an asset. At Saint Elizabeth High School, Jugy and I were put into a French immersion class predominantly made up of wealthy anglophones and children of diplomats. Here we were leaps and bounds ahead of students who were only just learning the foundations of the French language. It was a welcome relief from the trials and tribulations of the previous few years. Our transition to Ottawa was ultimately a smooth one.

It eventually became clear that André's whims had factored into Mata's decision to leave for Ottawa. He, like Mata, loved adventure and the excitement of new beginnings. I guess that's what made Mata gravitate toward him; like her, he was a person who liked to pack up and leave at a moment's notice. That said, we never totally understood why we had moved to Ottawa. Although we never respected André as a father figure, the more André was around, the more Jugy and I normalized his presence. Our indifference didn't make him feel uncomfortable around us. In fact, it often felt like he was *too* comfortable. He would try to act like a parent but without having the legitimacy, in our eyes, of a father figure. Looking back, our feelings were deep rooted; growing up without a stable father figure, we had high expectations for anyone who tried to assume that role. We didn't want to "settle" for someone simply because he was Mata's boyfriend. For this reason, André clashed with me and Jugy. It didn't help that when things got out of hand or when we talked back to him, he would just get up and leave. This was a recurring issue with André—he ran away when things got tough. But it was clear that he loved Mata, so he kept coming back. And Mata kept welcoming him with open arms. I wasn't sure why; possibly, he represented stability to her.

Even though Pita was distant, he found a way to stay connected to us. A few months after school started, he surprised us by giving us money to buy a computer so we could "keep up with the world." Pita, in many ways, understood the world through the "technology" he had access to: books, radio, and his conscientiousness. He knew that we needed more, and he saw the technological revolution that was increasing in our society. Without saying a word about his intentions, he had been saving up money for a few years. He was thoughtful. It felt like we were always on his mind, even when we didn't see him for weeks—or months—at a time.

In Ottawa we ran track and played basketball, competitive volleyball, and even badminton. Sports accentuated our friendships; we created bonds and began to feel at home. Then, in the blink of an eye, the school year ended, and Mata decided it was time to move. Again. These moves from city to city were becoming routine for Jugy and me. We had felt sad in the past when we had to leave friends behind. But now it was just normal. I started to think of relationships as temporary and therefore futile. Every time I integrated into the social fabric of a new community, I was taken away from it. Over time, I became independent, almost too independent. I could leave a friendship or relationship and never look back. And so when we left Ottawa, it was without a fight or any resistance.

FIVE

TEEN ANGST

In early July 1998, Jugy, Mata, André, and I moved to Dorval, a suburb on Montreal's West Island whose demographic mix was reflected in its mix of residences, from the massive houses along Lakeshore Drive to social housing projects to retirement homes for the elderly. Though the class differences were wide, overall the community was a quiet one (other than complaints about the airplane noise) where most people kept to themselves—being too busy with work, child care, or school.

In terms of the distribution, political affiliations, and education levels of its population, Dorval was similar to the "redlined" communities created in the wake of the suburbanization of the United States after World War II. Decisions about housing, development, and schooling reflected the desire of the white majority, leaving minorities with unfavorable housing conditions that contributed further to their racial stigmatization.

Mata was able to afford a three-bedroom apartment, which meant that Jugy and I, for the first time since our arrival in Canada in 1993, no longer had to share a room. This was a major step. Now, thanks to Mata's grit and hustle, mixed with disciplined saving and some help from André, the fridge was always full, we had nice clothes, and life was better and more comfortable.

To this day, I wonder what it must have been like for Mata to feel such financial pressure, especially being the mother of hungry twins who longed for a worry-free life. The older we got, the less aware we became of her struggles, financial or otherwise. This wasn't for a lack of care or interest, but because, over time, we got everything we needed. Mata made sure of it.

ALTHOUGH I APPRECIATED THE WAY Mata cared for us, I was becoming old enough to better understand the implications of her absence when we were kids. I'm still uncertain if it was my age or the subconscious pain, but when Mata would put her arm around me, I would give it a gentle nudge and wiggle away. Ultimately, that little boy chasing her car when she would escape in the wee hours of the morning never forgave and never forgot.

"I am really sorry for leaving you, boys," she would lament.

"Ah, Mata, relax, we had an amazing childhood," I would answer, trying to absolve her of her regret. But Jugy, being the pensive twin, would never answer. The reality was that her absences hurt us, subconscious or otherwise. Clearly, she knew that we were hurt, but in her defense, the reality was she knew that she was leaving us in good hands, in a beautiful community surrounded by nature and spirituality. In many ways, I felt like I had the best childhood a kid could ask for, with all its flaws and imperfections. But Mata did not see it like that. She never forgave herself for leaving us.

In the early hours of the morning, Mata's screams of despair and horror pierced through the walls of our apartment on a regular basis. She had reoccurring nightmares that her little boys were gone or somehow taken away. Except now we were in our late teens. "Oh mon Dieu! Jugy! Bala! Jugy! Bala!" she'd yell in a panic before dashing into our rooms to see if we were still there. "Mata, you're dreaming! You're dreaming!" I'd yell back to get her to snap out of her trance. After a few seconds of panic, she'd calm down and go back to bed.

The nightmares were something we never discussed. They were normalized because they occurred so often. In some ways, Mata was more scarred than we were. She'd lost her mother at a young age, and when she had us, she left us, and that tormented her, even in her dreams.

MY BEDROOM, A DECENT-SIZE WHITE RECTANGLE with wooden bookshelves surrounding my frameless double bed, faced the parking lot of the building. Only a couple of stories up, our unit was one of the few that was close enough to the outside world to feel grounded, yet vulnerable. The seven-foot-high chain-link fence that ran the perimeter of the building, visible from my window, made me feel caged. Looking down, I could almost make out the heavy locks meant to assure car owners fearing late-night break-ins.

About a hundred yards away from our apartment were a series of tall brown buildings arranged in a U-shape. One day, I hopped the fence to check them out. As I approached the compound, I saw clothes hanging off balconies, waving like white flags in the summer breeze, and heard children's voices both inside and outside of the buildings. Deteriorating brick and an unkempt lawn suggested that maintenance wasn't much of a priority. Nor was safety. I could have entered any of the buildings, if I had wanted to.

"Hey." Unsure if the greeting was directed my way, I kept walking. Then, against a wall, I saw them: a group of teenagers, some light-skinned, some Black, in baggy T-shirts and scuffed sneakers. "Welcome to Batshaw, bro," said one.

"I'm just passing through," I replied.

"Aren't we all?" he responded as I walked away.

Not knowing what Batshaw was, I was perplexed by his comment. It was only months later that Mata found out that it was a province-run group home for foster kids, disproportionately filled with Indigenous and other nonwhite children, called "racialized" children in Canada. Batshaw had no sports infrastructure and offered no community programming or supervision other than night guards and a few social workers who made sure the kids received three daily meals. Child protection? It seemed more like child survival-of-the-fittest. Batshaw was where I first recognized state-sanctioned neglect.

In many ways I grew up without parents; I was, quite literally, raised and nurtured by a village. I knew it was wrong for parentless children, or kids taken from their parents by the state, to be confined to what looked like a little prison where they didn't have access to nature and were not offered educational, spiritual, and worldly experiences like the ones I had had at the ashram. It was clear, even to a young outsider like myself, that these children lacked care and support. More shocking, it seemed the society I was part of was not bothered by their condition.

WHEN I LIVED AT THE ASHRAM, I had everything I needed to develop holistically. I always had access to books, nature, sports, and opportunities to quench my thirst for adventure and exploration. In Dorval, I was entering into a new high-school environment that was the exact opposite: it was going to limit my powers, drain me of my spirituality, and lead me off-track.

École secondaire Jean-XXIII was as bare-bones as it got. Classes were filled well past the recommended capacity, with a mix of middle-class and low-income kids who, I suppose, the province didn't care enough about to invest in. There were no social supports. At the time, and even today, Quebec's provincial educational system has the lowest salaries for teachers and the highest high-school dropout rates in the nation. Go figure.

The division between the school's administration and its students was immediately apparent. The teachers constantly screamed, "On parle français dans cette école!" ("We speak French in this school!"), whenever they heard English conversation. It was a French-language school, but I still struggled with the language, and policing how I spoke in the hallways aggravated me rather than inspired me to master it. Even today, Quebec-born francophones would rather enforce language laws and regulations then holistically allow newcomers and anglophones to appreciate and value their French culture.

Whether at school or in the streets, most people I came across spoke "franglais"—a mix of English and French with, depending on the person, some Arabic, Créole, or Spanish thrown in too. Linguistic diversity was not just normal, it was part of our way of life. But that way of life clashed with the principal, teachers, and staff members, who saw our slang as rebellious. This "rebellion" resulted in detentions, which merely served to fuel our hatred of the system. We often felt like rejects in our own school.

In the multicultural microcosm of Jean-XXIII, I found my crew *really* quickly. My closest friends were Mo, a Palestinian, and Garret, a Jamaican, both of whom immediately welcomed me into their inner circle. From there, I met Chris, a Dominican; Baron, also Jamaican; Milos, whose parents were from Yugoslavia (before it split); Lamar, who was African American; Ji, a Korean; Hussam, who was Egyptian; and Klaus, from the Philippines. Drew, the clown of the crew, was as white as they come. We were diverse. We fit together. As months, and years went by, we became more and more inseparable. After school we would go to the parks or basketball courts, or hang out at a strip mall we called Mega.

IF MATA HAD A GIFT FROM GOD, it was intuition. Shortly after moving to Dorval, sensing that Jugy and I were about to veer off-track, she enrolled us in a high-end theater school to take part in a play called *Le Bourgeois Gentilhomme*, written by Shakespeare's French contemporary Molière. There were, however, too many external factors in and around the school—poverty, drugs, fighting, social tensions, weak sports programs, and burned-out teachers—to keep us on-track. I was in an environment that would derail any teenager, even one with the potential to be an excellent student and a professional athlete.

In late July 1999, having just turned sixteen and about to start grade ten, I went to a party with the crew. We arrived at a house so packed with people that we could hardly move from room to room. Being somewhat claustrophobic, to get some space, I went in the kitchen. Cal, a tall, lanky friend of Baron's, was rolling a joint on the counter. I watched as he took out a bag of weed and some papers. He began to meticulously rip the buds into small pieces, and carefully put them on the counter. He sprinkled some tobacco on the weed and mixed it all together before evenly laying it out in his rolling paper. As he rolled it all together and licked, sealed, and twisted the joint shut, it felt like a ceremony. It wasn't just about getting high; Cal was in the zone, enjoying the process. My curiosity was piqued. Taking a worn-out black lighter from his jeans pocket, he lit the joint and passed it my way.

"I don't smoke," I said.

"But bro, it's just a plant," he laughed. I hadn't ever thought of it like that. Pot was still illegal. In the news and the movies I saw, it was portrayed as dangerous and smoked by druggies and vagabonds. Everyone around me looked foolish yet cool, and "integrated." So I stood there thinking about it while the joint made its way around the circle and back to me.

"Pass it over," I said. And I took my first puff.

At that moment, I became as foolish as everyone else in that kitchen. Maybe smoking weed was inevitable. It was abundantly available. I wasn't on a sports team, had no job, and, quite honestly, no vision for the future. Yes, I had freedom of choice and autonomy; however, the environment I was in significantly increased the probability I would make that poor decision. To this day, I'm not sure if trouble found me, or if I found trouble. All I know is that things started to rapidly spiral out of control.

ALTHOUGH MATA WORKED HARD to provide for us, we didn't have a lot of disposable income, if any. The idea of using Mata's hard-earned wages from health-product sales to buy "wants" rather than "needs" was out of the question. And so as Jugy and I grew older, we craved financial independence. We couldn't burden Mata with requests for new clothes or money to go out with our crew. The lifestyle we wanted came with a price.

One day after school, when our crew was hanging out at Garret's place, he started telling us about his "weed arithmetic": "I got twenty-eight grams, one ounce, for $200 bucks. I took that and made thirty-five 0.8-ounce dime bags I can sell for $10 bucks each."

We watched as Garret wrote it all out on paper, like the algebra problems we did in math class. "That means I can sell twenty dime bags to make my money back, smoke five, sell ten to pocket $100 bucks." Everyone sat in silence as Garret's bellowing laughter echoed through his unfinished basement. It seemed so simple, so easy. And he knew it. We all knew it.

So later that week I picked up my first ounce from Garret for $220. I guess he made a twenty off each of us. We didn't really care, though. We weren't after the big bucks—it was the thrill of getting some basic cash flow and smoking for "free" that kept us coming back. Calling a dealer, doing the pickup with friends, smelling it, weighing it, rolling it—we felt like businessmen. When we did have smoke sessions, we didn't use much: we were poor and didn't want to "smoke the profit," or as Biggie proclaimed on his track "Ten Crack Commandments" "never get high on your own supply." We would "put in" $2.50 each to get a ten piece. But even that was regulated: puff, puff, pass. It was the rule we lived by. Weed was shared. It was distributed. It was equal. At the end of the day, we were brothers seeking comfort, which many of us didn't have at a true home, and community, something we didn't have at school or in the surrounding environment. We weren't just homies, we were like family.

It didn't take long for people around the school, on the outdoor basketball courts, and in the local parks to learn that I had weed. I didn't think of myself as an evil "drug dealer," but rather as someone providing a product that should have been legal in the first place. While other people I knew graduated to selling QPs (quarter pounds), I stayed at the ounce level. I didn't want to get mixed up in the big game, and the money I made from the side-hustle was more than enough for my needs at the time. Keeping things small also helped me hide the "evidence" from Mata, although I'm sure she knew what we were up to. If she got home before I had a chance to open the windows and clear the air, she'd yell, "Ça pue!" ("It stinks!") from the front hall. Jugy and I just ignored her. Cracking a window and doing our homework was enough to satisfy her, so we took full advantage of it.

The more we sold, the greedier we became. Our judgment was clouded by the money, financial freedom, and the minimal *power* that we gained from the hustle. For the first time in my life, I felt like I was in control of my own destiny, steering my own ship. Years of poverty and vulnerability seemed to vanish with each sale. We were pushing past the things that had previously contained us, or at least we thought we were. As amateur drug dealers, we were not equipped to protect ourselves in the streets. Unbeknownst to us, street gangs would "tax" small dealers like us. They saw themselves as the "government," with the right to tax businesses, control the block, and monopolize violence. I never got taxed, but my boys did. We all knew the rule, in the event of taxation, you took the loss and moved on to live another day. And it was pretty simple— they would ask to buy an ounce, and when shown the product, they would just take it.

My standards for myself were distorted. My vision was to have a black Mercedes-Benz, an ounce of weed, a cell phone, and "Hail Mary" by Tupac blasting through my car speakers. Those were my personal standards; it was no surprise that such ambitions would only lead me down the wrong path.

Z WAS THE "DAREDEVIL" OF OUR CREW. He hung out with us, but we all knew to watch out for him. He was bigger than us, being a year older, and had been selling for longer than us. He had influence.

"You never got your stash back, eh?" Z asked one of my boys after he was taxed.

"Nah, but it's all good. I rebounded," our friend replied, nonchalantly. He had graduated to QPs and had enough supply to get back on-track with his business. He was always levelheaded and calm.

"That ain't right, though," Z insisted. He seemed angry, which neither of us understood. "We have to get even," he continued, pressing harder.

"I don't need the headache, Z. It ain't worth it. Chill," our friend repeated. But Z, apparently, had plans. I'm not sure why he was so set on "getting even," but his tactics played on my impulsivity and protective instincts. I disagreed with my friend, even though I was seeking to protect him.

Z set up a "hit" in some apartment buildings at the north end of the city that were a ten-minute walk from Mega. He told me to meet him at the building's fire exit at 8 p.m. There, he laid out our plan: he would run upstairs with pepper spray while I waited at the base of the stairs, ready to rob the dealer when he emerged from the building. Without asking questions, I agreed. For once, I could be the "government." I could be the top dawg. *Why was it always us little dudes getting taxed and punked?* I thought to myself.

We met at the agreed time, and Z went up the stairs while I waited at the bottom. At first, all I could hear were Z's footsteps echoing through the stairwell as he climbed higher. Then, all of a sudden, he was yelling and running back down toward me. When he came into view a few seconds later, Z was pulling the dealer by the arm. I froze. Z hadn't told me which dealer we were messing with, and in that moment, I realized I should have asked.

It was James, a kid from my gym class whom I had played ball hockey with just a few days earlier. This wasn't anonymous anymore. It was personal, and I was exposed. Instead of sticking with

Z's plan, I instinctively moved out of the way so that James, who had managed to release himself from Z's grip, could run.

"What the hell was that?" Z screamed.

"Z, that was James! He goes to our school . . . what were you thinking?" I couldn't believe it.

In that moment, I knew that my intuition had been right, and this wasn't worth it. My weed dealing had gotten out of hand. It was a dangerous game to play, even at lowly street levels. My life was so far off-track that I hadn't even felt myself fall off the rails. I viewed dealing as a social- and a financial-facilitation tool, an easy way to gain and maintain a basic level of autonomy. Young people like me were falling through the cracks, not because we were *bad boys*, but because we didn't have the avenues to express ourselves positively and meet our fullest potential. I hadn't realized that dealing was contributing to my own marginality, that it was affecting my safety and, ultimately, my future. I needed to reorient myself and get back on-track.

AT THE BEGINNING OF THAT SCHOOL YEAR, Jean-XXIII had merged with a neighboring high school. Facing serious budgetary issues and a complete lack of social support, Jean-XXIII was already hanging on by a thread when three hundred additional students arrived in its halls. The "low-income" education we were receiving was put under even more stress. Nothing in the curriculum was inspiring, and the teachers were burned out, and underpaid, and skated by without much institutional oversight.

That year, many of us—including myself—failed grade ten. I didn't view studying for exams as necessary. I spent most of my time with Mo and Garret and the rest of the crew playing ball, rapping, and smoking in bus stops or local parks. The day we found out we flunked, we were smoking when two cops rolled around the corner. I crushed the tip of my joint and put it in the front pocket of my hoodie.

The officers, one young and French, the other older and Italian, walked toward us.

"What do I smell? Give us the weed or you'll be arrested," they said, searching the vicinity for evidence.

"I don't know what you're talking about, officer," said Garret, locking eyes with me. But I couldn't lie. For some reason, in good faith, I trusted the cops when they told us we wouldn't be arrested if we handed the weed over to them. I also wanted to avoid any escalation.

"Here," I said, pulling the joint out of my pocket and placing it into the open palm of one of the cops. I had barely pulled my hand back when he started to yell.

"Turn around and put your hands behind your head!"

The next thing I knew, I was in the back of a police car in handcuffs. I pleaded with them to let me go but was met with silence. My heart raced. I saw my future going down the drain. I was being treated like a criminal, but I was no criminal. I was simply lost on my journey, disconnected from my passions. With little self-respect and low expectations of myself, I was wasting my potential, acting like a fool. I had just flunked out of high school and was smoking weed with my friends. It wasn't the cops who were about to flush my future down the drain—that was on all me.

"Please. My mom is going to kill me. I want to go to college one day. This is going to ruin my life." I pled my case to the cops, knowing that if I got in front of a judge, I'd be toast.

Although I'd had very little personal experience with law enforcement until then, I knew, thanks in part to my favorite rapper and revolutionary, Tupac, that racialized young men like myself were often bullied by the criminal justice system. In the 1980s and 1990s, rappers were exposing raw social realities instead of glorifying drugs and violence. For better or for worse, when I was growing up, I learned more about life from rap than I did from my teachers at Jean-XXIII.

I guess my tone and manner were enough to show the cops that I was genuinely remorseful and truly repenting. So when the older Italian cop stepped out of the passenger seat and opened the back door for me, he immediately unlocked my handcuffs.

"Quit that stuff and go back home," he quipped, setting me free. In that moment, I realized how thin the line was between success and failure. I'd been playing with fire and could quite literally have ruined my future simply by smoking a joint.

The criminalization of minor drug use and possession in the United States and Canada, known as the "War on Drugs," disproportionately affected young Black men. In fact, before the legalization of cannabis, Black people without criminal records were three times more likely to be arrested for cannabis possession than white people, despite consumption rates being nearly identical. The "War on Drugs" in both countries led to the overrepresentation of Black and Indigenous men and women in prisons for drug charges, a reality that we still face to this day.

In 2018, the Liberal Party of Canada campaigned on legalizing the simple possession of cannabis—and won. Despite its legalization in Canada, and in parts of the United States, inequity still exists as criminal records were not expunged. In both countries, the majority of cannabis business owners are white, in part because of the historic impacts of the "War on Drugs." With US sales of cannabis expected to reach more than $24 billion as of this writing, the industry, and government, has profited handsomely from the history of exclusion and prosecution of people like me. The government, just like those gangsters who would tax and intimidate us, controlled the industry with an iron fist, disciplining anyone who disobeyed by monopolizing power and violence through the police and courts.

BEFORE MY RUN-IN WITH THE POLICE, Pita, like Mata, had noticed a deterioration in my behavior and lifestyle. But even though I spent little time with him—I would see him maybe a couple of times a year, if that, and never told him that I failed grade ten—he was able to see right through me. Over time I began to "rock" baggy jeans, oversize tees, and what Pita called "silly caps." While there was nothing wrong with my fashion, it was alien to my father, who had sported a button-down shirt and tie throughout his schooling in Jamaica. A strict man who never minced words, he often told me to not act "like a n———." In fact, when we went for walks near his apartment in Montreal, he would give me long lectures about it. He was clearly worried. But the longer those lectures got, the more I would interrupt.

"You need to learn to shut up and listen," he would retort, sternly.

Pita saw that I was off-track, and he was trying to pull me in. I was truly lost and didn't even know it. I was ignorant in the face of my disorientated life. I was disconnected from my roots. Because Pita wasn't around, my reference point for what it meant to be a Black man wasn't my father but the representations I saw in media and music.

THE MAJORITY OF MY crew AND I planned to go to an adult education school in Montreal to finish high school. The Place Cartier Adult Education Centre taught its courses in English. On the surface, this seemed great—especially since my low grades in French class were the catalyst for my high-school failure. Place Cartier, though, was a breeding ground for the same bad behaviors and habits that I'd taken up at Jean-XXIII. There were hardly any "real" adults there; rather, it brought together all the students who had failed in surrounding high schools and those from across the island who didn't speak French but were too poor to attend English private school.

And yet studying in my first language also made it clear to me that I could excel in academics. At Jean-XXIII, I was taught a flimsy curriculum in a second language. It felt like being forced to drive an old station wagon but still being expected to "keep up with the world," as Pita would say. Every year in the United States and Canada, more than a million students drop out of high school. In low-income areas the number can be double the national average, if not triple, which begs the question: Are students failing high school, or is high school failing students? I think it is the latter.

Studying in English was no silver bullet, not even close. On our breaks, I would still bum a cigarette or smoke-up with my friends. I hadn't yet given up my bad habits and lifestyle. After failing and retaking a few exams, I was still lost and off track.

EVERY SUNDAY, I WATCHED NFL FOOTBALL, like millions of Americans and Canadians—a Sunday tradition. Once, when the players were being introduced at the beginning of a game, I heard the commentators call out the name of a five-foot-eleven, 180-pound defensive back. There was nothing flashy or notable about the player, but I couldn't help noticing that we had the same weight and height. Our physical similarities, coupled with the fact that I used to play football in the grassy pastures of the ashram, made me think, "I can do that."

The next day at school, I told my friend Klaus I wanted to go to college to play football and that I was going to become a professional football player. Klaus wasn't as surprised as I thought he'd be. He knew that sports and I went hand in hand, but he still sarcastically replied, "If you say so." At that point, though, it didn't matter what anyone said to me. I was ruthlessly ambitious when I had a target, and football was now, suddenly, my aim. The path was simple: finish high school, get to college, play ball. But to do it, I needed to get my act together. The epiphany energized me, gave me a sense of urgency. Just like fighting, I thrived under pressure, and pressure, at that point in my life, was exactly what I needed.

And so, with some grit, and a sprinkle of academic focus and determination, despite all the troubles, the ups and downs, I successfully completed high school. Given all that I had been through since arriving in Canada, it felt like a victory.

THE SUMMER BEFORE JUNIOR COLLEGE—called CEGEP, unique to Quebec, with a two-year curriculum equivalent to grade twelve that offers a bridge between high school and university—the crew was dreaming big; we had drive, and we had ambition. Ideas began circulating about us joining the Canadian Reserves. I would rant about playing professional football. By the start of summer, it seemed somewhat promising, but our environment was the same: little to no activities, no sports infrastructure, and no coaches or mentors. It became a summer like any other, one of partying, playing basketball, and being our rebellious selves. As the long summer days drifted along, so did our respective dreams. By my eighteenth birthday, my football epiphany had faded to a flash-in-the-pan idea. As a "gift" to myself, I smoked a dime bag. My pockets were as broken as my dreams. Jugy didn't talk much, but he was observant and courageous. While we all talked and talked, he planned to actually join the Canadian Reserves. For Jugy, the Reserves were not just about easy money; joining would be his saving grace, making him feel motivated and purposeful.

Although Jugy passed the Reserves summer program and continued to serve on weekends, by late fall, a month after our eighteenth birthday, I noticed his behavior began to change. He spent long hours in bed despite my efforts to draw him out. I am not sure whether it was the trauma from our childhood, the drugs, or his experience in the Reserves, but it all weighed on him in silence, at depths I didn't understand. This was devastating for me— I was confused and concerned. We'd all been smoking weed, but it seemed to affect Jugy differently from the rest of us. He didn't talk about it. He didn't share what was going on in his mind. He was suffering, and there was nothing I could do about it. It was excruciating.

SIX

SAVED BY FOOTBALL

Misguided and reckless, a summer of getting drunk and high was not ideal for getting ready for a football season, let alone CEGEP. Nonetheless, the plan was to attend John Abbott College on the western tip of the island. On football registration day, I told my crew that I wasn't going to sign up.

Even *they* found my hopelessness unacceptable. "You've been talking about pro ball nonstop. Go!" they said.

Deep down I knew I needed to break from my bad habits. And even though I didn't owe them anything, I thought back to the cops who'd let me go because of my claims about wanting to go to college. I'd been given a second chance and needed to capitalize on it. So one summer morning I jumped on the bus and took the forty-five-minute trip to John Abbott.

When I arrived for sign-up, the football team's head coach, Dennis Waide, looked me up and down and said, "You're going to be our running back." But as a gifted biracial athlete in a majority white school, I had no intention of being the team's workhorse: I had my own dreams.

"Nah, Coach," I told him. "I'm a DB" (defensive back). My tone and assertiveness signaled that I was a man on my own mission, or a hard-headed kid. Regardless, Coach Waide let me be and accepted without saying too much. He knew that if I was undisciplined and wild, the team's standard, structure, and routine would straighten me out.

Day one of training camp, a week before the start of school, was pure bliss. We did some sprints, footwork drills, and tackling drills. My aggression was expressive and my grit abundant as I propelled my body, helmet, shoulder pads into anyone in front of me. It was practice, but for me it felt like game day. Despite a few bruises and a headache, I felt great. After practice Coach Waide came up to me and said, "You showed spunk today, kid, keep it up!" I didn't know what that meant, but I had the feeling that he saw potential in me that was worth developing. Just like the guidance I had from the swamis when I was in the ashram, Coach Waide, like every football coach I would have, was taking on the role of both coach and mentor.

Thinking back to the rage I had during the tackling drills, it was as if the frustrations I had toward society and my life were channeled on the field. Football was the perfect outlet for my emotions and a great springboard to uncover my hidden potential. I could communicate my primitive feelings of passion and aggression through speed, strength, and power. The football field felt like home.

WITH FOOTBALL AS THE NEW CENTERPIECE of my life, smoking and hanging out with the boys became less of a priority. The schedule was a challenge. I needed to wake up at 7 a.m. to arrive at class by 8:30. Attending college while living at home with no car meant taking hour-long bus rides, surviving on granola bars and peanut butter sandwiches until practice at 6 p.m., and then hopping back on the bus at 8:30 p.m. to go home again. It was a grind.

On those long bus rides, I would see the modified sports cars of

the rich West Island kids fly by. Being broke and carless was aggra-
vating, but football—as long as I kept doing just well enough aca-
demically to be eligible to play—was keeping me on-track. It wasn't
just about the discipline and the rigorous training; it was the dream
of possibly playing professional football that was keeping me focused
and motivated. In fact, during my second year, we won the Bol d'Or,
a provincial championship title. In my third year of a CEGEP program that most students graduated from in two, I was unanimously
named an all-star, having led the league with eight interceptions.

IN 2004, HALFWAY THROUGH my third year at John Abbott, I was
ready to start focusing my sights on bigger and better goals. I was a
few credits short of graduating and attending a university in Quebec,
but I had amassed enough credits to attend a university outside of the
province. The education system in Quebec was complicated, but it was
also a blessing. If being a few credits short meant I had to leave the
province, so be it. I didn't know how it would all work out, but I was
motivated to follow my dreams of playing pro ball. My coach asked
me to attend a "combine"—a recruitment camp where all the top
Canadian universities selected their players. I was so excited about
the prospect of showing off my skills that it didn't even occur to me
that being selected at the combine would mean I'd need to apply for,
get into, and pay for university. I just wanted to prove myself at a new
level—a level that separated "good" players from "great" ones.

Hundreds of athletes were at the camp, which was held in the
spring, when the weather was still cool. We were all being evalu-
ated by coaches, who were intensely watching our every move as we
were tested in running, lifting, and a series of drills. I was comfortable in these high-pressure situations. The more pressure, the better. I never shied away from a fight, and in that moment, I felt like

I was fighting for my dreams. I ran a speedy forty-yard dash and excelled in the bench press. I got offers from a range of universities across Canada, but it was Denis Piché, head coach of the University of Ottawa Gee-Gees, who caught my attention. "You were on fire today," he said after searching me out in the crowd of athletes leaving the field. "You have big potential, and with the right team around you, we can do great things together."

The more he spoke, the more it felt like he knew me—my past struggles, my trials and tribulations. Being from Montréal-Nord, a rough and rugged neighborhood, Coach Piché recognized my potential and knew that he could help me flourish with the right guidance and structure. So when he offered to take me on with the Gee-Gees, I informally accepted without considering how I would actually make it happen. I let my excitement get the better of me. Attending U of O was a long shot: I didn't have money, and Mata didn't either. And the truth is, going to university was beyond what I imagined possible for myself, let alone a university in another province. I had ambition, but I didn't know how to elevate myself out of an environment where I was continually exposed to weed, cigarettes, and partying—an environment, in other words, that lacked resources to help me meet my potential. Pita was the only person in our family who had gone to university, but I didn't feel that I could turn to him. I was stuck.

Although I felt ready for this next step, the more I thought about it, the more unrealistic it seemed. I continued to smoke weed, and the more I did, the more I felt I needed to let my football dreams go. After weeks of trying to figure out how to get the money I'd need for tuition and rent, I decided I couldn't make it work. So without saying a word to Coach Piché, I decided not to apply to U of O. I didn't want to entertain the prospect of being accepted and not being able to say "yes." I took myself out of the game so that I wouldn't have to face that reality.

..

IN THE SUMMER OF 2004, before our twenty-first birthday, Mata told Jugy and me that she was leaving Dorval to move to a "pictur-esque cottage" in the Laurentian Mountains, a rural area an hour northeast of Montreal. All the work Mata had done through the years had finally paid off, and she clearly needed—and wanted—a break from city life.

"What are we supposed to do, Mom? We have no money for an apartment!" I said. Over time, we had transitioned to calling Mata "Mom" and Pita "Dad," but not just because we were getting older. We saw the names "Mata" and "Pita" as spiritual ones, and since we had drifted away from our faith, we didn't feel connected to those names anymore. So "Mom" and "Dad" it was.

"You can stay at your father's place," she calmly replied.

I suppose it was justified. We were men. Plus, she'd cared for us from the moment we arrived in Canada in 1993, while Dad had taken very little responsibility. And Jugy and I were no longer chil-dren: we were twenty-year-old men, smoking and partying with friends. She needed her space.

"Call your father," she said, as Jugy and I stared at her blankly.

"But Dad lives in social housing," Jugy replied. "In a one-bedroom."

"You'll have a great time, and you'll make it work. You have a week. Pack," Mom said as she hugged us.

For reasons she never explained, Mom and André had split just a few weeks before her move. He left without saying goodbye to me and Jugy. André must have gotten tired of moving from place to place. At the end of the day, our mother was on another level. She was an ambitious, energetic dreamer. André was a spiritual but mellow guy who, like most people, lacked Mom's fire. Once again, just like she did with Dad, it was time for her to live life on her own terms, without anything or anyone getting in the way. My mom's lifelong sense of adventure and free-spiritedness makes me believe that people never change. They go through life, evolve and grow, but deep down our essence remains the same.

I tried my best to see the bright side of the move—Jugy and I had been separated from Dad for years, only seeing him on weekends here and there throughout our high school and college years. Perhaps this would be good for our relationship, perhaps making it stronger; we would get to know each other better.

But reality set in as soon as we arrived at his place. His social housing unit was six hundred square feet, with a bedroom, living room, and bathroom. The tightness of our living quarters was exacerbated by the piles of books and clothes that Dad kept in nearly every square inch of the apartment. Jugy and I made it as comfortable as we could by moving his stuff around; we made our respective beds with boxes, books, and cushions.

Wanting to be out of the apartment as much as possible, I spent most of my time with the crew. Nights, we would drive around downtown Montreal in my friend Ji's Chrysler PT Cruiser. One humid August evening in late 2004 we met up with plans to "pregame" at the open plaza in front of Place des Arts, Montreal's premier performing-arts space, before going clubbing. It had been our weekend tradition for the last few years. But when we drove up to park in our usual spot, we found cement barricades about six feet away from each other, blocking one of the entrances. Baron suggested parking the car in a nearby alley and jumping the barricades. Being young and feeling invincible, the rest of us agreed.

The slam of car doors rhythmically boomed like timely bass to the ruckus of the busy street, as did our laughter as we prepared to take on the "wall." I put down my wallet, cell phone, and keys. I wanted to get a running start to propel myself over, but just as I was about to jump, I clipped my foot on a raised cement platform.

I flew through the air, somehow making a spectacular landing on my feet. Everyone erupted in cheers.

"Holy shit, that was crazy!" Ji yelled as I swerved back over to the group.

Later, after we'd finished our drinks and smoke session, we walked down the street toward a local *dépanneur*, or corner store. As we waited to pay for our munchies, I realized I had left my wallet, cell phone, and keys back at Place des Arts. We raced back, but by the time we got there, everything was gone. Damn. I had no choice but to go back home.

Without my keys, I had to ring the bell. It was around midnight. Dad answered, clearly pulled out of sleep by the shrill buzz that echoed throughout the apartment. The deeply pronounced bags under his eyes accentuated his disappointment. Normally he would have given me a long speech about what I was doing and where I was going wrong. But this time he simply sat down in the darkness, his back turned to me, and rumbled, "What am I going to do with you?"

With those words, my life changed forever. For years, Dad's lectures had fallen on deaf ears. I thought he was trying to control me. Despite the fact that I admired and respected his intelligence and profound wisdom, I didn't see him as a role model. He lived in social housing and had few friends, so why should I listen to him? But hearing the regret in his voice, I realized I was too far down the wrong path. I was twenty-one years old, irresponsible, undisciplined, unemployed, still didn't have a CEGEP degree, and spent my time clubbing, drinking, and getting high—all while living with my dad. I had gotten to a point where he didn't even want to try anymore. He didn't see any reason for making the effort to explain to me what I was doing wrong. It was clear that he thought I was too far gone. But I didn't want it to be that way. I respected Dad, even though I didn't often tell him that—I knew I needed to clean up my act. That night I made the decision to never smoke weed again. My commitment, firm and true, until this very day.

A FEW WEEKS LATER, while sitting on Dad's sofa, I got a phone call just after 11 a.m. from Coach Piché.

"Where are you?" he asked impatiently. "Training camp has already started!"

"I'm at home in Montreal. I didn't apply to university. I didn't work all summer, and I have no money."

"What the hell are you talking about!? Get your ass down here! I'll get you into a program. You'll apply for a few jobs at the sports center, and I'll make sure you have a place in residence." It was like a gift from God. Still, I'd become so apathetic that I was momentarily speechless. Living with Dad and Jugy in such cramped quarters had stunted me mentally even more than it had physically.

"Let me talk to my mom. I'll call you back in a minute, Coach."

My mother was my rock. If I needed something, or wanted advice, I called her. She was the single most reliable person in my life.

And so I called her, curious about what she would say.

"Bala! C'est fantastique!"

"The thing is, training camp has already started, so I need to get there as soon as possible," I said.

"Pack your things. I'll come get you tomorrow morning and we'll be in Ottawa before noon!"

It took my crew to push me to sign up to play football, Coach Waide to give me an opportunity, Coach Piché to swoop down like an eagle and rip me off my dad's sofa, and Mom to give me that final push out the door. Despite my apathy, the universe seemed to be conspiring to help me.

SEVEN

MY REAL EDUCATION

The University of Ottawa was just what I needed. For the first time in my life, I had my own place to live and days filled with classes, work, study, and football practice. I'd never had so much structure before: it was so new that it felt empowering. I was back on my journey, a man on a mission. In fact, it was the first time since the ashram that I found myself in a setting—academic and athletic—conducive to my growth and development. Back in Montreal, Jugy was doing better, which gave me peace of mind. He had graduated from CEGEP with excellent grades, had a girlfriend, and was going to attend McGill University's physical education program.

And yet, with a mix of combativeness and ego, I still managed to get my own way.

On my first day of football training camp, the captain of the team asked me where I had gone to college to play football.

"John Abbott in Montreal," I replied.

"You know that's a double-A school, right? I went to a triple-A." I couldn't believe that the person who was supposed to be the team's leader was trying to cut me down the first chance he got. He didn't even know me.

With enough ego for the both of us, I didn't back down.

"What're you tryna say?" I asked. But before things could escalate, Coach arrived, and we started our drills.

The captain clearly hadn't liked my tone, though. So on rookie night—a party for the new players hosted by the upper-year players that was more of a frat-style "initiation" than anything else—he decided to get me back. Right after I arrived, he pressured me to drink a mix of whiskey and beer, followed by some crackers and hot sauce. As I was puking out this "poison," all I could hear over the loud music was his yelling: "That's right, boy! That's what you get!" It didn't set things off on the right foot.

Weeks later, when I told my coach that I wanted to go into human kinetics and health science, he confused me by saying, "You're more of a black-and-white kind of person." He put me in leisure studies, which, as far as I could see, wasn't going to lead to much of a career beyond being a park ranger. Motivated to get out of that program, I took courses that would allow me to transition into health science and biology. The following summer, I took math courses at a local high school that would make me eligible for university-level calculus.

Between practice and classes, I began to think more critically about academia. The more I read, the more I noticed flaws in the university curriculum. I was expecting inclusiveness, enlightenment. Instead, I found the exclusion, homogeneity, and white power structure that I had been experiencing my whole life.

I took a human geography course called "Contested Places" that looked at urban planning in various areas of Canada, including Ottawa-Hull. When I asked the professor why there was no mention of Black people in the studies he had given us, he dismissively replied that there was simply no literature on the topic. Not only was he trying to brush me off, he didn't want to concede that there were problematic gaps in his course content. Throughout my life, seemingly small events have often had a tremendous impact on me. My brief exchange with that professor, who was blind to exclusion in his course content, lit a fire within me. This time, I would use that fire, that energy, to empower me along my journey.

Visiting Montreal during the Christmas break was like stepping into a time machine. I felt like both the city and my crew were frozen in time, unchanged during my absence. Without community role models or an inspiring environment, they were stuck. I didn't judge them for it; after all, I had experienced the same thing. Stagnation is too often the reality for youth in Montreal. Despite what was occurring in the classroom, Ottawa provided me with a stable and safe space to grow, away from the negative influences and worldly desires that Montreal had pressed upon me.

I SPENT A COUPLE of WEEKS of my break with Jugy and Mom at her cottage: an airy, spacious, three-bedroom bungalow with tall windows and a fireplace. It was good to spend time with both of them, but especially Jugy. Since I'd left for U of O, his mental health struggles persisted and, mostly owing to distance and my busy schedule, we'd fallen out of touch. In my absence, Mom's unconditional love was Jugy's protective cloak. Their mother-son bond was strong, helping him cope despite experiencing the same social exclusion that my father continued to live with.

Jugy and I then spent a couple of days at Dad's place in Montreal before I headed back to Ottawa. One morning, I took a walk along Saint-Catherine Street downtown: the snow was piled more than two feet high and the sun was shining brightly, reflecting off banks that hadn't yet been trampled by pedestrians or cars. There were barely any people out, so I had the sidewalk to myself. In the silence, I started thinking deeply about my life, how far I had come and where I was going. I thought about my place in the world relative to my socioeconomic situation and identity. I questioned why people who looked like me and who'd grown up poor so often went down the route I had: selling weed, craving material items, and excessively identifying with rap and hip-hop lyrics. More often than not, it didn't end well. Why were people who looked like me overrepresented in prisons and underrepresented in school curricula? Why were people who looked like me underrepresented as elected officials and in executive positions in the private sector?

If I could break the cycle of poverty and marginalization in my own life through sports and education, couldn't I help others do so? Education, it struck me at that moment, could be the "great equalizer." I was aware that higher education influenced everything, from income to the likelihood of staying in a marriage to one's exposure to violence. In my mind, it was then, during that slow walk down Saint-Catherine Street on that cold winter day, that I realized that education was the way I was going to rebel against society and launch my personal revolution to improve and empower myself. Education would become my shield and sword that would empower me to improve myself and redesign the world around me.

There are countless examples of minorities struggling to attain quality education, and I didn't want to be yet another one. Historically, in the antebellum American South, it was illegal to teach Black enslaved people to read, let alone "allow" them to go to school. States like Missouri banned education entirely for Black people. Some Canadian provinces had segregated schools as well. In the United States and Canada, high schools still fail minorities with their limited resources and crumbling infrastructure, and although Canadian colleges and universities don't collect race-based data, there are indications that they are exclusionary and less accessible to minorities.

Despite their historic disenfranchisement, however, my Black ancestors proved to be resilient. To get around Missouri authorities who didn't want to see freed slaves like himself learn to read, John Meachum, in the mid-1800s, equipped a steamboat with desks and a library and called it the Floating Freedom School. In 1960, Ruby Bridges, the first African American child to attend a white Southern elementary school, had to be escorted to school by US marshals to protect her from violent mobs. They stood up against a system that had cast them out. As I began to read more often, and better understand history, the words on the pages began to inspire me.

IN MY SECOND YEAR OF UNIVERSITY, I decided I wanted to move away from leisure studies and into health sciences so I could become a health and physical education teacher. Sports and education had changed my life, and I wanted to "pay it forward" by helping other "lost boys" like I had been. I believed that most at-risk youth had simply gone astray on their journey and needed a mentor, teacher, or guide to put them back on-track.

When I told my academic advisor my plans, he told me that I was better suited to an easier program. I wasn't sure what he meant. *Is he really telling me I'm not smart enough?* I asked myself. I thought back to my eighteenth birthday, when I'd smoked that dime piece as a "gift," how low my standards for myself had been. Now I was sitting in front of a university-level academic advisor who was, intentionally or not, imposing low standards onto me.

Viewing my education as an act of rebellion, all it took was for someone to challenge me. After that conversation, I successfully completed biology, precalculus, calculus, statistics, and ten health-science courses. I was well on my way to being a health and physical education teacher. With education as my rebellion, against all odds, I was making inroads.

AFTER SPENDING THE FOOTBALL off-season training and working for a moving company, I arrived in training camp in top shape. Once practices began, it was clear that I was developing well within my athletic prime. But during the first game of the season, I smashed my head into an oncoming running back, leaving me with a serious concussion. Following concussion protocol, I was ruled out of play for a week. The next game, my teammate Tafari and I sat in the stands, drinking vodka we'd smuggled in. Our team was losing, and, like idiots, we started acting wild, heckling players on the opposite team, unaware we were surrounded by alumni and our rivals' parents. They certainly knew who *I* was, though, since I was outfitted in the team tracksuit.

I was summoned into Coach Piché's office the following day.

"Were you drinking in the stands during the last game?" I knew that the answer I was about to give him would have serious consequences. Despite my shortcomings, I've always been brutally honest, almost to a fault. So I understood that in this situation I would be punished by the truth, but I couldn't hide what I had done.

"Yes, Coach," I replied, looking right into his eyes. He paused, but his eyes lasered back at me. He turned red. After a few seconds, he cleared his throat.

"Get out of my office." I wasn't sure how to feel about his reaction. It seemed like I'd gotten off scot-free, which almost made me feel worse. Like Dad, Coach Piché seemed too disappointed to put any effort into disciplining me.

The next day, I ran onto the practice field in my gear: shoulder pads, helmet, and gloves. About ten yards into my jog, Coach Piché walked in front of me, yelling, "Get off the field!" He pointed to the locker room. I halted in confusion.

"Get off the damn field!" he yelled again. He could have told me I was suspended when I was in his office, but he purposefully hadn't. I suppose he wanted to make a point and use me as an example for everyone else on the team.

Following close behind me was Tafari, who'd also been sent to the locker room.

"What was that?" he asked me, but I didn't reply. On our way to the locker room, I heard footsteps in the hall and knew it was Coach, coming to talk to us.

"I expect you here every practice. But you're not playing. You're sitting on the sidelines, watching the people who care about this team. And you're going to learn from them," he explained. I had no choice but to listen. I couldn't fight back, especially since I had been in the wrong and had, quite frankly, brought this situation on myself.

"This is not the hood. So act accordingly."

I couldn't let one mistake define the rest of my university career and, honestly, my life. But Coach Piché wouldn't budge.

Coach Piché made us run laps and simply watch from the sidelines as the team practiced and prepared for weekly games. I could tell he wanted me to stay in shape but still had to teach me a lesson about professionalism and self-respect. During the last week of the season, after I had attended practices for more than seven weeks, Coach Piché offered me an opportunity to return to the team. But he still wasn't going to let me off easy.

"If you're going to be a part of this team during the playoffs, you have to make amends to your teammates," he said. "If they want you here, and think you can bring value to us, then you're welcome back."

After practice the next day, when everyone was taking a knee in the middle of the field, I was given an opportunity to speak.

"I apologize for poorly representing the team and my overall be-havior. I love the game, I appreciate you all as teammates, and I ask that you allow me back on the team." My teammates looked at each other, eyes darting around. I was transported back to middle school, when my classmates had whispered to each other when they heard my unfamiliar name. My teammates would be the judge and jury. Whatever they decided, I had to abide by.

Our captain stood up after a minute of deliberation: "Alright, fine."

And that was it. He didn't seem particularly excited. But I'd been granted another lifeline.

In that moment, I finally understood what Coach Piché had been doing for me. I thought his punishment was harsh, but he was teaching me a lesson bigger than football, one I would carry closely for the rest of my life: *self-respect*. My behavior in the stands, drink-ing and acting like an out-of-control vagabond, was reflective of the mistakes I'd made in the past—behavior that had led my father to ask what he was going "to do" with me. In suspending me, Coach had echoed Dad's frustration while also showing me how to have self-respect by setting high standards for myself and expecting me to live by them day to day. It took a whole village to raise me in New Vrindaban, and now it was taking a whole football team.

In July 2006, RIGHT BEFORE the start of my third season with the Gee-Gees, I was hanging with my roommate Arlond in our seventh-floor apartment. Luzo, a six-foot, 250-pound heavy-weight from Nigeria, had come from out of town to chill with Arlond. He had a boastful arrogance that didn't sit well with me. He was loud and obnoxious and always looking to get people riled up. On this occasion, in classic Luzo fashion, he started a conver-sation about slavery, culture, and US history. I expected the worst before he even opened his mouth, and the worst was what I got. His claim was that Black Americans had "robbed" *real* Africans ("from Africa") of what it meant to be Black because of how "they" acted and behaved in America.

"It's hard to be an African in America because of other Black Americans," Luzo blurted out.

"You are aware that Black Americans are a) from Africa and b) responsible for abolishing slavery, the civil rights movement, dominate music, culture, etc.? What the hell are you talking about?" I responded. But Luzo wasn't having it. He was the type of person who was deaf to anyone who disagreed with him. After he threw out another faulty argument, I decided to disengage from him, but being stubborn and never one to back down from a fight, I still wanted the last word.

"If it wasn't for African Americans, Black people, to this very day, would be enslaved. Your mother, sisters, and cousins would be abused, raped, tortured, and lynched. That's the reality, Luzo. You can't deny that." Before I could finish, Luzo stood up from his chair and moved toward me.

"Man, what're you doing?" I calmly said as he got closer. "If you have an issue, we can go downstairs and settle it."

"Let's go," he responded, breathing heavily. He backed away so I could get up from the beanbag chair where I was sprawled.

"I don't want to hear about any of this after, understood?" I said. At that point, I was no longer angry about the debate. He was so clearly in the wrong that I should have just laughed at his non-sense. But I wouldn't tolerate someone trying to intimidate me in my own home. So we took the elevator to the ground floor and went to the park across the street to "settle" our differences. Luzo, who had height and weight on me, put up his hands as if he knew how to fight, but he clearly didn't. After a jab, followed by a slew of windmill punches, it was over. Luzo was bloodied and floored. As Arlond tried to calm a hysterical Luzo, I just stood there with a throbbing pain in my hand. I looked down, and sure enough, my thumb was out of place. I had swung so wide that one of the punches had landed on the side of Luzo's thick head. I suppose mine was thicker for taking on this fight.

A trip to the hospital and an X-ray confirmed the obvious. It was like a repeat of my high-school days: I'd suffered the exact same injury for the exact same reason. Football was supposed to begin in a week, but now my season was over before it had even begun. Instead of building on my power, I'd gotten too tied up in my emotions and let my ego and aggression get the better of me. I wasn't a boxer or a professional fighter; I was a football player and a student. I'd just shot myself in the foot, by breaking my hand, again.

THAT WAS MY LAST FISTFIGHT. It took years, but thanks to my time in Ottawa, and the support of my coaches and teammates, I eventually managed to pick my battles, and stay out of trouble. Our phenomenal 2006 season ended with our winning the Ontario Championship, the Yates Cup. But when we lost at the next round, one game away from the national championship, I was devastated.

I knew I would need all my energy and power to realize my dream of playing professional football. Football is all about speed and agility, especially when you're a defensive back. To survive as a DB, you need to be the fastest person on the field, or you'll get eaten up. So after that season ended, I decided to try out for the university track team. When I showed up at the four-hundred-meter indoor track known as "the Dome," I was greeted by the coach, Glenroy Gilbert, an Olympic gold medalist in the 4-by-100-meter relay and a University of Ottawa alumnus. I didn't know it then, but track would become my solace and refuge. In track, there are no politics, just gravity, time, and the laws of physics. There's no need to get along with a captain or to deal with other players. It's just you against the clock. And getting on the team is simple: if you have speed and power, you're in. Running track would also allow me to follow in my father's footsteps. The many gifts he bestowed on me included athletic ability and, most of all, speed. I had a superpower that I was about to unleash.

With his mere presence, Coach Gilbert set high standards for the team. Athletically, my mind was set regarding life after graduation: Plan A was to get drafted into the Canadian Football League (CFL); Plan B would be to try out for the Canadian Olympic track-and-field team. Once equipped with a university degree, I would apply for a master's in sports administration. If I took one lesson away from my years at the University of Ottawa, it was that no matter how hard things got, how many suspensions, concussions, broken bones, doubters, and naysayers I faced, I could defy the odds as long as I didn't quit on myself. With a bit of determination, and a pound of perseverance, I had created the athletic and academic opportunities that would allow me to continue on my journey of growth and discovery. The next stop on that journey? The CFL Combine.

WHEN I ARRIVED AT THE COMBINE in spring 2008, I was in my prime. I ran a 4.4 in the forty-yard dash, could bench press 225 pounds fifteen times in a row, and excelled in one-on-ones. As at the university combine where Coach Piché had recruited me, I wasn't the biggest or the tallest, but I definitely was the fastest.

Following my performance at the combine, I was signed by one of the CFL's top agents, who saw my potential for going pro. The Winnipeg Blue Bombers had called Coach Piché to chat about their draft pick, and they were focused on another player, but just as he had done from day one, Coach Piché directed them toward me. I owe a lot of my success to Coach Piché. He believed in me, he pushed me, and he looked out for me. He gave me my wings.

Being signed as a free agent to the Blue Bombers was a huge accomplishment, and it was just the beginning. I still had to prove myself in training camp and preseason games. But I had confidence. For the first time in my life, I felt like I was at the pinnacle of my abilities. My mind was clear and laser-focused. Training camp, which was held at the Blue Bombers' stadium in Winnipeg, was grueling; it felt like a two-week-long fistfight. But I enjoyed and welcomed the confrontation. And I excelled. The receivers voted me best rookie DB. I was picking off balls in practice, and I was thriving. I was going one hundred miles an hour with every drill, earning myself the nickname "Grinder." In my first preseason game, on my second play, I jumped a dig route and got an interception. I was in the zone.

I was walking back to my hotel across from the stadium at the end of preseason when the phone call came from my agent: "You officially made the team!" I jumped with joy and excitement. Just like Mom, from the moment we arrived in Canada, I had hustled. I was a fighter. By week one of the season, my fight was as fierce as it was on the first day of training camp. Running down on kickoff and making tackles made me feel like a ferocious lion.

In Winnipeg, a teammate and I rented rooms from a family who lived in a nice house about a ten-minute drive to the stadium. In early September, a few hours before one of our games, there was a knock at my door. Without telling me, Dad had driven more than fourteen hundred miles from Montreal to come see my game. I couldn't believe it.

"Wow! Dad! What if I wasn't home!?" I laughed with amazement.

"Well, you are, aren't you," he said with his signature smile.

Dad was always thoughtful and supportive, and he loved to surprise me and Jugy. He wouldn't talk about it—he'd just do it. Unlike
Mom, I don't think Dad felt guilty about leaving us at the ashram
because he did not have a say in it. Also, he knew something special, a secret, that he never told me but showed me through his
actions. From the day we were born to the moment we left for the
ashram, the unconditional love he showed us was so powerful that
it was etched into the memory of our DNA, in our subconscious.
Despite being separated for nearly a decade, in his presence, over
time, his love, through deliberate actions, reminded my soul of the
love he has had from the day we were born.

LIKE MY MOTHER HAD ALWAYS SAID, football is dangerous. It's
a physically demanding sport and, quite honestly, a violent one.
Although I had had decent luck over the course of my career when
it came to injuries, that luck soon began to wear off. In my first
off-season, I went to Jamaica to do some training, and to get away
from Dad's cramped quarters where I was living, and tore my
meniscus while playing basketball. I returned to Canada, got an
MRI, and had surgery about three weeks before training camp,
which I survived—barely.

Running down on kickoffs, my specialty, had its ups and downs:
it was exhilarating and exciting, but there was a high likelihood of
injury, especially when an incoming player—often a larger one—
would run toward me at full speed. In my second season, in a game
against the Montreal Alouettes, I tore my shoulder after a brutal
collision on kickoff. With my family and hometown friends in attendance, I didn't want to walk off the field, so I stayed strong until
halftime. I'm not sure if my choice to stay in the game exacerbated
the injury, or if it was bad from the get-go (maybe a bit of both), but

the tear ended my season, requiring surgery and a six-month rehab program. Injuries in football were simply the nature of the beast, something I had to deal with.

Over the course of the rehab program, I had a lot of time to reflect. After just two years, I was ready to make a change. It wasn't that I didn't like playing for the Blue Bombers; I did, but my heart was in a different place, and I couldn't see myself living in Winnipeg for a decade. Not long after my season with the Blue Bombers ended, I called the general manager of the Montreal Alouettes, Jim Popp, and told him I wanted to play in my hometown. The team was coming off a championship win against their biggest rivals, the Saskatchewan Roughriders, and had their sights set on back-to-back Grey Cups. My whole life had been about experiencing different environments, some enriching, others not so much. What I wanted was to be back home in a championship environment.

Two days after the call, Popp invited me to a recruitment combine, where, as with all high-pressure situations, I excelled. Twenty minutes later, I was signing a contract on the trunk of the scout's car in the parking lot of the Lachine sports complex. It was a dream come true.

I was on-track to have a great off-season. I wanted to prove to Coach Marc Trestman and the whole Alouettes establishment that they had made the right choice in signing me. I grinded, day in and day out, ate healthy, ran track, did yoga, and got at least eight hours of sleep each night. I was at the top of my game. I had been living with Dad—my salary as a Canadian professional football player simply wasn't enough to cover rent *and* all of my other expenses. But, as when I was younger, his apartment wasn't healthy for me, but it was especially problematic for a professional athlete. After four months of training and hibernation, I needed an escape.

On March 11, 2010—I remember it like it was yesterday—I was

invited to my friend Drew's birthday party. I planned to have a couple of beers and then head home to get ready for a track session the next morning. Instead, we ended up "popping" bottles and I woke up late with a hangover. As soon as my eyes peeled open and I saw the red numbers on my alarm clock, I regretted my "decision." Being late for practice isn't an option for any athlete, especially at the professional level. It's seen as disrespectful to your fellow players, coaches, and the team as a whole.

Panicking, I ran as fast as I could to the metro. As I entered the station, I heard the subway car pulling up to the platform. I swiped my card and sprinted down the stairs. Near the bottom, to avoid a man coming up the stairs, I jumped. It must have been at least seven steps. Pow! I landed awkwardly on the platform. By the time I had untied my shoes to take a look at the damage, my foot had already doubled in size. I managed to hobble onto the metro and get to speed training, where I showed my coach my swollen foot. His "you're screwed" look said it all.

When the doctors and physiotherapists I consulted were unable to effectively diagnose my foot, I went back to Ottawa to consult with Dr. Greenburg, one of the country's best sports medicine doctors. The news wasn't good. According to the physio, I had a potentially career-ending Lisfranc injury—a fracture in the midfoot area due to torn ligaments. It might require surgery, but certainly a boot. I was devastated. If my foot was broken, my dreams were, too. My first training camp with the Alouettes was only eleven weeks away. I had worked way too hard to go down like this. Failure simply wasn't an option. I knew that if I told my coach about my foot, I would be cut from the team—that was just the reality of being an athlete in the pros, let alone on a team of defending champions. If I couldn't perform, I would certainly be replaced. I wouldn't let this injury, quite literally, break my legacy.

My stress began manifesting in unexpected ways. I would wake up in the middle of the night, drenched in sweat, hardly able to breathe. I felt like I was back in the ashram's sweat lodge, panicking at the heat and pressure surrounding me. I needed to tap back in to my meditation. I needed to be calm. I needed to breathe. Otherwise, this injury, and my deteriorating mental health, would destroy me and my career. I needed to inhale the confidence and exhale the fear. I needed to help myself: even the best physio programs wouldn't work if I didn't. I needed to find my inner strength—the strength I had as a young boy in that West Virginian sweat lodge, surrounded by swamis with unwavering mental fortitude. That was how I was going to survive.

As weeks went by, the swelling decreased, but I still wasn't able to run. With only a few days left before training camp, I visited Mom at her new apartment in the Plateau, an area of Montreal. She had the running shoes I'd used for track at the University of Ottawa, and I wanted to use them to "test" my foot. I laced up and headed to the alley behind her rowhouse. Breathing heavily, pumping myself up, I took my first strides and, much to my surprise, found the pain manageable. I couldn't believe it. Smiling, I walked back into the house.

"So how did it go?" Mom asked, the moment she heard the door open.

"I'll survive training camp," I responded, with a grin.

Although I was a little rusty from lack of game play, I not only survived, I made the team.

But I was in survival mode, on and off the practice squad. The battle wasn't just physical; it was mental as well. By the end of the season, I was getting more play time. It was only in the final week of the Grey Cup that Coach Trestman selected me over another player who was meant to be on the roster for that winning game. My dream of being a Grey Cup champion with my hometown team came true that November in 2010.

WINNING THE GREY CUP wasn't just about football; it was about overcoming a lifetime of challenges, being resilient through obstacles, and holding myself to high standards. My injuries, family challenges, and personal struggles had tested me, but I weathered the storm and survived. If I could tap into the lessons I learned at the ashram, anything was possible.

The championship also gave me a sense of closure. My heart was no longer in football. I had accomplished everything I set my mind to. As a young, scrappy man answering Coach Piché's call from my Dad's makeshift couch, I never would have guessed that just years later I would be a Grey Cup champion. The CFL had been great to me, but I knew that there was more to life than playing football.

IN 2011, WANTING TO GIVE BACK to the Montreal community, I began coaching youth in sport. I started Bala Athletics, a start-up training program for student athletes. Youth in Montreal, especially those who are racialized or live in low-income neighborhoods, often suffer from severe inequality, racism, and social exclusion, especially when they're deprived of social support and positive role models. If anyone could attest to that reality, it was me. I had nearly fallen down the wrong path but was saved by my mentors, role models, and an inner fire.

For two years, I ran Bala Athletics to provide guidance and resources to youth who were growing up like I had, to support them in setting goals and overcoming challenges, and, at the most basic level, to show them that someone cares—that they matter and belong.

If I was able to overcome my own obstacles, I knew the youth I worked with at Bala Athletics could overcome theirs too. I wanted to inspire the next generation to take up a positive revolution and rebellion just as I had done. My gravitation toward coaching and mentoring youth reminded me of the swami's prediction when I was in New Vrindaban and my mother's definition of a guru. I can just hear her voice, "they're leaders, mentors, and teachers who help guide people." My role as a coach at Bala Athletics not only put me on a path to fulfill my destiny as a guru, but it was also a vehicle to empower the next generation to positively rebel and meet their fullest potential. The lessons from the swamis, Mata, and Pita, along with the life experiences I had acquired, were helping me to develop into the person I wanted to become. With Mata as my rock, Pita as my compass, and Jugy as my companion, the world was at my fingertips.

EIGHT

A MOTHERLESS SON

It was a cold morning in Montreal, January 1, 2013—the beginning of a new year, which in years past had brought me a sense of renewal, resolution, and rejuvenation. Waking up just past ten o'clock, I looked at the snow that had accumulated on the rooftops of neighboring buildings. I felt safe, hidden under the thick duvet Mom had given me for Christmas just a week before. The quiet buzz of my clock radio hummed in the living room just outside my door, nearly muted by the sound of children playing in the snow in the park across the road from my building. That morning would be the last time I would feel at peace for years. It was the calm before a storm I wasn't prepared to face.

Waiting for my coffee to brew, I admired the light that beamed in through the floor-to-ceiling windows in my condo. It seemed as if the heavens had opened, parting the clouds so that the sun could cast its magnificent golden rays over the world. The yellow hue, reminiscent of the temple in New Vrindaban, transformed my concrete ceiling into a majestic work of art. It was my own spiritual retreat in the heart of Montreal.

Meditating on the new year and my aspirations for the future, I thought about Jugy, Dad, and Mom. After multiple injuries, and my heart completely out of football, I attended football camp with a level of disinterest that would get any player cut. My passion for the game had faded, and it showed. Upon my release from the team, I felt free. With my championship ring in hand, it was time to embark on a new journey. I was looking forward to a fresh start and to begin building a life for myself outside of sports. I looked forward to continuing my work with Bala Athletics, paving a path for future generations, but I also had my sights set on going back to school. I had big plans, and I was ready to take them on—until my life got turned upside down.

The call came from Bob, Mom's brother.

"Bala, your mother's in the hospital," he said. "She has a viral infection that's clogging her lungs. You and Jugy need to come to the hospital." Her missing spleen had finally taken its toll on her body. The organ produces white cells and antibodies, so those who lack it are more susceptible than others to infections, including the pneumonia now ravaging her lungs. I could hear the beep of a heart monitor in the background while Bob explained what was happening to Mom. It was hard to focus on anything except the high-pitched noise that I knew was mimicking my mom's heart-beat. It was slow.

Sitting in the waiting room, I could feel my heart racing. Jugy's leg was bouncing up and down, rubbing against the side of my parka. As the brushing grew louder and louder with each movement, my anxiety grew stronger and stronger. I was trying my best to meditate, to tap into my inner strength, but my breathing was superficial. It was almost as if my body was involuntarily replicating the pain Mom was feeling in her room down the hallway. Every minute that passed seemed like an eternity, but the hospital reception clerk had insisted we wait to speak to a doctor before going in to see her.

"Balarama? Jagannatha?" We heard our names called out from across the room. We stood as the doctor, who was oddly dressed in black, made her way toward us.

"I'm afraid your mother has contracted a serious viral condition that's causing her lungs to fill with fluid." Jugy and I stood in silence. I could feel the capillaries in my cheeks begin to surface and my blood pressure rise. I broke into a cold sweat. "She's unable to breathe, so we've put her on a ventilator to help hold her lungs open and ensure that her air sacs don't collapse. When you enter her room, you'll see a series of tubes around her face, and a plastic mask covering her mouth. She won't be able to speak." She paused, her eyes scanning mine, then Jugy's. "This is a normal course of action for patients in this position."

I was afraid. I didn't want to see my mother at her weakest moment. My heart beat quickly as Jugy turned to walk toward her room.

"You go first," I whispered to him.

"Why?" he responded, clearly surprised at my hesitancy.

"Tell me what it's like before I go in." Jugy seemed confused, but he obliged. I could hear him breathing heavily until he entered the room, which was filled with the pumping sound of the ventilator. After a couple of minutes, Jugy stuck his head out of the door.

"Bala, come on. It's okay." I beckoned him into the hallway. I wanted to know more before I took the plunge.

"She's swollen," he said, "and you can tell her breathing's bad—she's almost blue." I didn't know what to do. "Bala, trust me, Uncle Bob's in there too. It's okay."

I went into the room with my arms hanging loose, my body limp. My feet moved me toward the bed, but my mind and body were stuck, aching from the pain radiating through my heart. I grabbed Mom's left hand, and Jugy, walking to the other side of the bed, held her right. Her long fingernails were painted with a sheer coat of light pink metallic polish. I rubbed my thumb against hers. I could see the remnants of mascara on her eyelashes. The ends of her hair were still slightly curled.

The longer I stared at her, the more foreign she seemed. I was losing touch with the person I loved. Despite the ventilator mechanically pumping oxygen into her lungs, I could feel her soul leaving her body, floating up to the heavens that had opened this morning, as if for her. As I began to speak, her eyes fluttered. Her grip tightened around my hand. I told her I loved her. I thanked her for what she had done for me. I reassured her that she was safe and that things were going to be okay for us. I knew she was listening, even in her most vulnerable moment.

The next day, the doctor called me with an update on our mother's "status"—it was all so clinical, as if she were a medical apparatus instead of a person.

"Your mom is in critical condition, and it seems like her breathing is getting worse. Her reliance on the ventilator is nearly 100 percent." As the doctor spoke, our eyes were widening with each word.

"At this point, it's a matter of time."

"How much time?" I responded, cutting off the doctor before she could say anything else.

"Between twelve and twenty-four hours. I'm deeply sorry."

It was hard to believe that my mom's life was being quantified in hours: a life that had been so rich and so adventurous might be ripped away before the day was over. It was brutal.

As we re-entered Mom's room, it was clear that the end was near and, honestly, I hadn't thought that was possible.

"We're going to need to make a decision about your mom"—

the words I didn't want to hear. I didn't want her life to be in my hands. I didn't want to make the wrong decision. But after a few hours of discussion, the answer seemed inevitable: Mom needed to come off the ventilator. We didn't want to prolong her suffering.

"My deepest condolences." At the doctor's words, I burst into tears. I couldn't fathom never hearing our mother's voice again, never sharing meals, never seeing her dance, never listening to her stories, never laughing with her, never crying with her, never hugging her, never again telling her "I love you."

We weren't the type of family that often expressed our love for each other. In fact, I could count on one hand the number of times I had told Mom, Jugy, and Dad that I loved them. It wasn't that those feelings weren't there, but we didn't feel the need to express them. We showed our love by being there when we needed each other. But although I was where I knew I should be—by Mom's side in her last moments—I felt helpless. Words still needed to be spoken—words I should have said years and years before, feelings that I should have shared, thank-yous I should have said. I felt like I had been robbed of time—time to heal, share, reminisce, and rekindle.

Sitting in the hospital's waiting room, I felt numb. We'd informed the doctor of our decision. Now we were waiting for the nurses to arrive and to shut off the machines. I was afraid to see Mom in her final moments.

"You should be with her," my cousin pushed me. "You'll regret it if you aren't." Reluctantly, I walked the short distance to Mom's room.

"I love you, Mom. I love you." I couldn't muster the courage to utter anything else. The words I wanted to say escaped me as tears flooded my face and memory. I was in a state of shock and trauma.

Losing my mother was like losing a piece of myself. We were cut from the same cloth—adventurous, ambitious, fiercely independent, and spiritually minded. All of my openness, curiosity, and ambition came from her. All of my strength did too. And, in the moment, so did my weakness.

I stood next to her as she slipped away.

I CALLED DAD TO tell him the news.

"Mom died," I blurted out. Tears flowed down my face as I tried to catch my breath.

Dad's first word was, "What!?" He hadn't known Mom was in the hospital. Then there was silence. Waiting for what he would say next, I felt so depleted, I was barely able to hold the phone up to my ear. It felt like the heaviest thing in the world.

After a long pause, he said, "She is liberated." Though I knew he had strong beliefs in reincarnation and karma and accepted the inevitability of death, it still felt like Dad was treating Mom's death as a little too spiritual. This was real life to me, it wasn't time for spiritual life and death lessons. I stayed on the phone for a few more seconds. Dad didn't say anything else. I mustered, "Bye, Dad," and hung up.

My vision of the world was very different from my father's. As far as I was concerned, our mother wasn't liberated: there could be no freedom in her death. Unlike Dad, I was attached to the life I knew, attached to my mom, and attached to the comfort she had brought me, despite our ups and downs. My father was immensely intuitive (spiritually speaking) but rarely showed emotion. I believe he never really forgave my mother for taking us away when we were younger, so his emotional ties to her were limited. Even after her passing, he continued commenting and complaining about Mom, to the point where I stopped talking to him for nearly a year.

CLEARING OUT OUR MOTHER's apartment made her death a reality. We hadn't spent much time with her there, so the space didn't evoke as many painful memories as it might have, but it still smelled like her perfume, as if she'd been there just minutes before. It was clear that the last time she had been there she'd left in a hurry—her coffee mug still sat on the kitchen counter, half full. A plate with toast crumbs and a peanut-butter-smeared knife were left on the table.

"I'll start with the books," I said to Jugy as we planned how to make the agonizing cleanup as quick as possible.

"I'll take the kitchen." Luckily, Mom didn't have a lot of material possessions, so we figured we could be in and out within a few hours.

In her bookshelf, Hope Edelman's *Motherless Daughters: The Legacy of Loss* stood out for being so worn. Its pages were folded and creased, there were comments in the margins, and passages were underlined in pencil. Losing her mother at such a young age had made Mom fragile. She'd felt abandoned, just as I felt in that moment. And although I was much older than she was when she lost her mother, looking at that book resonated with me. A motherless son. I could hardly believe it was true.

As hours and days and weeks and months went by, I felt empty. This, the ultimate abandonment, was like an out-of-body experience. It took me back to the ashram, when I was a young boy running after her car shouting "Stop!" at the top of my lungs. Like then, I wanted to make her stay with me. But I couldn't.

We held a celebration of her life on Wednesday, January 9, 2013,

at a little reception hall. Nearly one hundred people attended, a reminder of the strength and support Jugy and I had in our community
and of the power and influence our mother held in her circles. As
an entrepreneur and life coach, she inspired hundreds of women to
embrace their truth and follow their hopes and dreams. She was
a beautiful woman, inside and out—one who helped others raise
their voices and succeed.

My mother is constantly on my mind. She may not have been
the perfect mom, but everything she did worked out perfectly for
me. And although she left this planet too early, her soul and her
spirit live on. She would often tell me, with confidence, that she
was going to live a long life, so when she passed, I felt robbed of
a future with her. But thinking back, I now understand what she
meant: she would live on through me. If being adventurous, taking
on any challenge with endless optimism, means that I am em-
bodying my mother's spirit, well that is exactly how I am going
to live life.

NINE

A JOURNEY TO THE EDGE OF THE WORLD

Throughout her life, our mother had been an avid adventurer, dreamer, a woman with a keen ability to mobilize people. In death, she inspired me to embody her vibrant liveliness. From the spring of 2014 through the summer of 2016, I left my comfort zone to travel, and teach, all over the world. I was yearning for a new beginning, but also for opportunities to heal, discover, and grow. The experiences of those two years allowed me to reconnect with the spiritual roots of my childhood, better understand the present, and propel my future in unexpected, exciting ways. Though I departed on my journey lost and broken, I would return healed and empowered, with a renewed vision of myself and the world around me.

It all began a few months after Mom's passing, when I applied to the University of Ottawa's one-year teacher-education program. From growing up in the ashram, guided and mentored by gurus, to being surrounded by books in my father's home, to coaching student athletes, teaching had always been an integral part of my life. Besides allowing me to connect with my deep passion for education, a teaching degree could be an escape out of Montreal, and eventually serve as a ticket for teaching abroad.

I was accepted into teachers' college and moved back to Ottawa to attend classes. The work was fulfilling and, in a way, comforting, too. Being surrounded by books at the library reminded me of being at Dad's house. The prospect of passing along to others the empowerment I was gaining was exciting. As a teacher, I would have the opportunity to mentor the next generation, to teach them how to not only empower themselves but to improve and enhance their communities.

After completing my teaching degree with a specialization in physical and health education and geography, I successfully applied to lead a group of University of Ottawa students on an international development trip to Costa Rica. Our tasks would include planting trees and teaching students from the local host school about sustainable water use and how to build and effectively use a compost system.

The countryside where we were stationed, just south of the Nicaraguan border, had a rugged austerity that appealed to me, partly because it conjured my childhood in the ashram. I had always cherished my memories of New Vrindaban and often tried to imagine what my life would have been like had I stayed there. Perhaps I would feel closer to Jugy. Perhaps my relationships with my parents would have never come close to mending. Perhaps I wouldn't have been left with a hole in my heart from the sense of abandonment that subconsciously I continued to struggle with. Perhaps I wouldn't have lost touch with my spirituality. But perhaps, on the flip side, my life would have been much less rich. Perhaps I wouldn't have realized my fullest potential and my life mission.

One day, as we were laying down red clay bricks for the compost system, I noticed local passersby staring at us from the road. Although I didn't understand Spanish, their tone suggested that they were questioning who we were and what we were doing to "help." This got me thinking: Was I really making a difference? And if I was, for whom?

People who go abroad to lead international development projects, people like me, tend to view their work as altruistic and beneficial to locals. But in that moment—when I was laying bricks *for* the students instead of *with* them—the sweat from my brow, and the reward I felt from working with my hands, getting dirty, and being productive, was actually helping me more than the locals. My volunteerism, I suddenly knew, was not about saving a community— it was about saving myself. They didn't need me. I needed them. Laying those bricks was like a natural therapy, a cathartic exercise to help me cope and overcome the loss of my mother, all while discovering the world and rediscovering myself.

After we had given a lesson on composting to the students and locals, one of the teachers, Mr. Marco, stayed to talk with us. We were impressed by the fact that he spoke nearly perfect English, despite living in such a remote village. Our conversation meandered, with Mr. Marco noting at one point, "In Costa Rica, we don't have an army. We don't need soldiers. Instead, we have students." To my surprise, that was the raw truth. I learned that Costa Rica's experiment with having no central military began in 1948 and stemmed from a desire to reallocate funds to education and health services. To this day, the country provides universal health care to its citizens and permanent residents. The World Health Organization has ranked Costa Rica's health-care system as number one in Central America and as the thirty-sixth best in the world. Its literacy rate, at nearly 98 percent, is one of the highest in the world, and its high-school dropout rate, at 22 percent, is significantly lower than that of Quebec, where nearly 36 percent of high-school students don't end up graduating on time, or at all.

The idea of investing in people rather than soldiers profoundly resonated with me. Since I grew up in a low-income household, it took years before I began to view education as a source of empowerment. With hundreds of thousands of youths across North America lacking proper housing, food, sports centers, books, coaches, and mentors, I started to imagine what might happen if our governments invested in students the same way they did in police and the military. From the city of Montreal, with 18 percent of its budget going to police, to the US military budget of $778 billion in 2022, metropolises and countries alike invest more in death than in the lives of the next generation. Maybe it is time we model ourselves after Costa Rica.

FOLLOWING MY TIME IN Costa Rica, I moved on to China—a mindboggling world of economic prosperity, worth ethic, and discipline—where I got various jobs teaching English to businesspersons and their children. My income vis-à-vis the cost of living allowed me to lead a very different life from the one I was used to in Canada. I had access to simple luxuries—tea, massages, dinners, and outings with colleagues. But what most amazed me was the respect I received from my students. In China, teaching is considered a "noble profession," and those who take on that role are seen as knowledge holders who remedy peoples' need to learn about the world. This gave me a new sense of purpose: I was admired and revered by my students, not disrespected and scorned like many

North American teachers (including those who had taught me in Montreal).

"Once a teacher, always a father," my students would say to me. The trust they put in me made me determined to give them the best possible education I could—the kind of quality education I had been deprived of for so many years but that I could provide to the next generation of leaders, businesspeople, and global citizens. China reinforced my emerging beliefs about the power of education.

VENTURING TO DUBAI AFTER CHINA was like stepping into another universe: Sand as far as the eye could see. Yachts docked in the clear turquoise water of the city's bays. Otherworldly architecture. Skyscrapers that reached the heavens. Innovation beyond belief. Men and women wore traditional Emirati garments. The United Arab Emirates was a land with deep cultural roots, yet excessive materialism.

Beyond the shiny skyscrapers and malls, though, it was clear that the city faced deep social, gender, and class tensions. Teaching was especially eye-opening in this regard: discriminatory legal and cultural norms were readily apparent within the classroom setting. My female students censored their views during oral discussions yet vividly expressed sensitive legal and cultural themes in their writing. Women have rights under the country's Personal Status Law, but accessing those rights is dependent on approval from male "guardians" who must grant women permission before they can vote, own property, or get an education.

I was distressed when I learned about these policies. My childhood may have been tumultuous, but I could say, with confidence, that Mom was always a strong, independent woman who couldn't—and wouldn't—be held back by any man. Even her relationship with André had been held on even terms, not his alone. Living in Dubai really put this into perspective for me. Although I had been critical of my mother for what I thought of as "selfish" behavior, in retrospect, I realized she lived life on her own terms. Most women in Dubai didn't have that luxury, despite the opulence of their city.

I rode four-wheelers through the desert to meet locals for meals in small cafes on the outskirts of the main city; I can still taste the flatbread and feel the warmth of it on my sandy fingertips. It reminded me of the food Dad made for me and Jugy for breakfast, served with lentils, chickpeas, and cheese. But I felt like I was losing touch with my roots, with my history and spirituality—a bit like Dubai itself, which had embraced a kind of hyper-Westernization. During the year I spent in that desert city-state, I realized that my ability to balance both worlds—the material and the spiritual—could make me powerful beyond my imagination.

SHORTLY AFTER I ARRIVED at my next stop, Malaysia, I made an early morning visit to the Batu Caves, a complex of grottoes that is a place of pilgrimage for Hindus. There—amidst the lush green forest; temples painted turquoise, pink, red, and green; tall limestone mountains; squawking parrots and rustling leaves—I felt immediately at home. Although initially unaware of the caves' Hindu connection, upon arrival I saw the golden statues of deities resembling those at the ashram, particularly the 140-foot golden statute of Murugan, the Hindu god of war and victory. Standing at the base of the steps that lead into the Temple Cave, the statue and its imposing scale humbled me: in that moment, I felt my insignificance in the world.

Surrounded by towering green trees and hundreds of macaques, I took my time climbing the steep, colorful stairs that lead up to the mountain cave. As I soaked in the landscape, I was transported back in time, not just to the ashram, but through Malaysian history. Hindus make up only a small fraction of Malaysia's population today, but many of the early kingdoms in Southeast Asia adopted aspects of Hinduism into their theologies, rituals, and architectural styles. Having grown up immersed in Hindu tradition, I was deeply touched by the locals and tourists who showed their respect to the faith.

Over the next two weeks, I visited a range of temples and spiritual spaces. As I did so, I reflected on my values and beliefs and considered how I could put them into practice in my everyday life. Free of any kind of itinerary, I let my spirituality guide me from place to place.

A few days before Christmas 2015, I left for Angkor, a temple city in Cambodia. My tuk-tuk driver got me there at dawn on Christmas Day, and I waited in line to enter the Angkor Wat temple. Despite the many tourists gathered there, you could almost hear a pin drop as the sun rose above the stone walls. It was one of the most beautiful moments of my life: as the orange sun cast its warmth over the site, the stone carvings that surrounded me seemed to come to life. The temple's thousands of intricate designs told thousands of stories; with each turn, a new set of floor-to-ceiling masterpieces revealed a history simultaneously foreign yet familiar to me. I gained a new perspective with each step I took, and was filled with peace and gratitude.

This was not the Cambodia that I, and many North Americans, had imagined. It looked and felt like a kingdom to me. But despite the scenic views—the lily ponds, rice fields, and tall palm trees—it was impossible not to notice the abject poverty that surrounded me. Even today, nearly 50 percent of Cambodian children are severely impoverished, without access to necessities, let alone education.

Heading back to my hotel, I came across an eleven- or twelve-year-old girl hauling a rusty oversize wheelbarrow that she was using to collect garbage. Her purple hoodie and red gloves were torn, and she wore a stained baseball cap to protect her face from the blazing sun.

I waved, unable to converse beyond a simple greeting. She smiled back, even though she was exhausted. But I didn't pity her; rather, I admired her work ethic. Throughout my travels, I witnessed ways of life that differed greatly from those of North Americans—people were proud of their jobs and the effort they put into them. They were diligent and unwavering in their commitment. This struck me as praiseworthy.

That Christmas Day in Cambodia was my second since my mother had passed, and I no longer felt connected to the holiday. Growing up, Jugy and I used to celebrate with her family, but after her death, we had lost contact with them. It was almost as if our familial bond had been held together by her joy and desire.

I could recall, the first Christmas we spent alone, Jugy and I ate lasagna, with Christmas movies playing on TV in the background. With the hum of the television making our silence feel less awkward, we sat at the dinner table, holding back tears, thinking about Mom. It was one of the most difficult days of my life. Since then, Christmas had lost its importance—it was just another day for me. And that Christmas Day in Cambodia was no different.

I WENT TO THAILAND and then to Egypt. It was 2015, four years after the uprisings in Tahrir Square in Cairo, when tens of thousands of Egyptians gathered to demand change. From Alexandria to Luxor, I was greeted warmly, as if I were a local. In some ways, I felt more comfortable in Egypt than I did in Quebec, where my golden-brown skin was a liability; here, it signaled royalty.

I taught in Cairo for a year, where terrorism, curfews, and limited freedom of speech were daily realities. Being culturally aware and politically cognizant were survival tools. In many Middle Eastern and North African countries, governments view the civil liberties we take for granted in North America as threatening to their leadership. This applies to tourists and visitors, too, who are wise not to think of themselves as exceptions, but to pay attention when the government gives orders.

On January 25, 2016, the fifth anniversary of the Egyptian Revolution, we were instructed to stay inside our dwellings. It was dangerous to roam the streets, even close to home. As I locked up for the night, sweat dripped down my temples. Although I would abide by all directives, the city's palpable tension made me uneasy. That day, Giulio Regeni, a twenty-eight-year-old student from Cambridge University conducting doctoral research on Egypt's trade unions was burned, beaten, mutilated, and ultimately murdered in a manner that bore the hallmarks of Egypt's security forces. Regeni defied their orders and lost his life because of it. For me, it was a strong reminder of the preciousness, and tenuousness, of democracy and security.

..

NEAR THE END OF MY TIME in Egypt, I went scuba diving in the Red Sea—the waters that Moses is said to have parted and whose deep turquoise color reminded me of my mother's eyes. I felt connected to her there, as if her soul were buried beneath the coral. With each stroke I took, I felt freer. It was like being reborn, baptized and cleansed in nature's holy waters.

After dinner and some rest, I made my way to Mount Sinai, where, according to the Bible, Moses received the Ten Commandments.

I and a few other tourists arrived at the base of the mountain at midnight, our plan being to hike to the summit by sunrise. We would travel first by camel, then on foot, stopping in caves for tea along the way. The closer we got to the summit, the closer I felt to my spiritual roots. As we followed the route taken by our spiritual forefathers, the mountain's silent aura felt powerful and majestic.

After hours of hiking, we finally arrived. The red granite rock glistened under the dim, glowing light of the rising sun. It was as if my body were being led back to my childhood. Standing on one of the world's most sacred sites, I felt humbled, connected to God, replenished. I felt whole again.

THE TWO YEARS I SPENT IN ASIA, the Middle East, and North Africa gave me a new perspective on life as well as the inner peace I needed to cope with my mother's passing. They also helped me cast my eye on my next project: making meaningful change in my hometown. The experiences I'd had and the people I'd met while traveling all enriched me and clarified my worldview. The global community I'd discovered during my travels had felt, in many ways, like family. It made me think about how Montreal might embody the same values of globalism, diversity, and inclusion that

I'd experienced in so many of the places I visited. I wanted to contribute to the creation of a community where anyone, regardless of where they were from or how different they may seem, would be accepted, just as I was across the world.

One thing I knew for sure: it was time to go back home.

TEN

THE RETURN HOME

My time abroad was a healing pilgrimage. The people I met, the mountains I climbed, the deserts I crossed gave me a sense of freedom, personal growth, and empowerment. In discovering the world, I found a balm for my wounds and sorrow. I was also able to tap into the adventurous spirit my mother had gifted me. It felt like my travels had given me an alchemical power to shift from negative to positive thinking, whether in relation to my mother's loss or my frustration with the social, cultural, and linguistic tensions I lived with in Montreal. I felt energized to embark upon a meaningful new chapter in my life, a continuation of the journey I had begun overseas, with new mountains to climb and deserts to cross.

With the passing of my mother and distance from my father, I did not feel at home in Montreal. My connection with Jugy had also weakened; years of being away had caused a natural cooling of our bond. It felt like an empty shell, a place void of family and unity. A place where anyone could be marginalized based on language, religion, skin tone, or ethnicity. Channeling my mother's venturesome and ambitious soul, I made a decision: if I didn't have a home, I would build one. But not just any home: I would transform my hometown metropolis into a place that would feel like a home for all—an inclusive and welcoming place, just like that Bob Marley concert where my parents fell in love, where everyone could come as they were, where everyone was accepted. My mother would want me to build on her legacy by creating one of my own. She would want her memory to be channeled into constructive and positive change and creation. She would be my secret weapon, my guardian angel, my "coach from above."

My mother's spirit was coursing through my veins. My travels had also refreshed my view of Montreal: with my newly global lens, I could see that it was one of the most ethnoculturally diverse metropolises in the world. People from all the places I had traveled and countless others across the world had ended up here. But although our diversity enriched the city, the province, and the country as a whole, its institutions, democratic or otherwise, suppressed and marginalized those who were seen as different.

To RESHAPE MY CITY and build this home for all, I needed tools—and power. It had become clear to me that democracy, law, and community engagement weren't just the key pillars that determine the nature and character of a society; they could also be levers with which to transform it. If law framed and ordered society, and politicians determined who got what funding, then that was the power center in which I wanted to operate, to make the changes that I wanted for Montreal, my city and home.

I decided that law school would become the way I was going to rebel: I could fight back against a system that had deprived me of a strong education as a youth by getting a degree that would give me the tools I needed to reorder, redesign, and reform society. But I knew that people were the real driver, the real force behind social change. Getting a law degree and then running for office and mo-bilizing communities would be the seeds to building a sustainable grassroots movement.

I recalled an article I had read in Egypt by American professor Jean Anyon in a Cairo coffee shop titled "Social Class and the Hidden Curriculum of Work" that affected me deeply. It stated that students from lower social classes had poorer classroom ex-periences and were presented with weaker curricula, what I call "low-income information for low-income students." I thought back to my high school, where the resources had been scant and the curriculum mind-numbingly disconnected from how I was experi-encing the world. The teachers were burned out, and the school had limited supplies and few sports teams. My application to McGill Law was the first step in my rebellion against the system that had in many ways robbed me and other low-income kids of their futures by failing to provide quality educational experiences. I would empower myself through education, acquire the knowledge denied me in my previous educational experiences, and equip myself with the legal tools necessary to not only take on the world, but to create a more just, equal society. Since my early twenties, I'd had visions of people living on the margins of society revolutionizing the *game* by acquiring as much education and, ultimately, power as possible—especially those, like me, who were members of so-called visible minorities. I saw education as a way to mitigate poverty and social exclusion and increase the Black community's—which is to say, *my* community's—awareness of the world and its inner workings. And I wanted to be a role model for that type of educational rev-olution.

I knew that getting into one of the top institutions in Canada would be a challenge. McGill is considered by many to be the

Harvard of the North, with all the exclusivity that implies. (Despite a lack of data on the ethnic makeup of its students, it is common knowledge that McGill is both exclusive, and exclusionary.) Its law program, which combines the study of Canadian common law, Quebec civil law, and Indigenous legal traditions along with a range of international legal perspectives, was one of the best in the country.

ONE MORNING, WHILE I WAS SOAKING in the heat of the sauna at my gym in downtown Montreal, I struck up a conversation with a man in his early twenties. The gym catered to an upper-class clientele—many of its regulars were middle-aged businesspeople and their children—so I wasn't surprised when, after I asked him what he did for a living, he told me he was attending McGill Law.

Though he fit the mold of a typical law school student, I didn't sense, throughout our conversation, any particular spark or drive in him. He seemed average, mediocre—further proof that privilege doesn't necessarily allow the cream to rise to the top. The more we talked, the more it struck me that if someone like him, who seemed so sheltered and lackluster, could be admitted to one of the best law schools in the country, then surely I could too. I had worked too hard and overcome too many obstacles, let alone having had attained three degrees and a variety of substantive life and travel experiences, to be denied. In that moment, it became abundantly clear to me: much like this gym, law school catered to wealthy white folks who lived in postal codes that gave them access to high-quality education from birth. Their skin tone, financial capital, and social networks gave these people education and power, which, once grasped, they held on to. Paired with a growing understanding that power is not given, but rather taken, my ambition to get into law school became even more pressing. It was as if my mother's spirit were driving me harder and faster than ever before.

For nearly four months, I sat in coffee shops and libraries, pen and paper in hand. My time, energy, and focus were now fully committed toward my new goal. I put countless hours of work into my application, and wrote dozens of drafts. I wanted the admissions committee to hear my voice in every word. I wanted to leave nothing to chance. My lifestyle became rigorous, monastic. Renting out my condo through Airbnb at that point was my only source of income. With Dad still in social housing and Jugy now living with his girlfriend, I slept in hostels while my condo was rented. When they were full, and any hotel I could afford was booked, I slept on the cracked cement floor in the basement of my condo building. I would simply lay down on the clothes and pillows I had stored in my locker, sleep until 6 a.m., and then use the showers at my gym to get ready for each day. The austerity made me feel alive, just as it had in the ashram. It also gave me a sense of continuity in my life's journey. The closer I felt to achieving my objective, the more the cement floor became comfortable. I was embracing the grind and my journey of change.

JUST FIVE DAYS AFTER submitting my application to McGill Law, Donald J. Trump was elected president of the United States. It felt like the whole world, including Canada, was in a state of shock. I was depressed. How could an openly racist, misogynistic man become the most powerful leader in the world? It was demoralizing.

Oddly enough, while I was in Egypt, I had often heard people hoping Trump would get elected so that "America could no longer hide from themselves." For them, Trump's overt racism and character would shine a light on American inequality and oppression, which had been obscured by Barack Obama's charm and grace. Trump represented the real America, a place whose ugly underbelly would finally be exposed by his victory.

At the time, I viewed Trump's election as a step backward. His populist rhetoric was allowing a resurgence of bigotry and discrimination. I was particularly concerned that the populism and nativism his election had unleashed would come to Canada and that Quebec, with its long history of ethnocultural/linguistic chauvinism, would be particularly susceptible to it. I felt with new urgency how important it was that every Quebecer, including myself, use their role (in my case, in law and politics) to push society toward equity and liberty; otherwise, what had happened in the United States would likely happen in Canada.

I was especially alarmed by Trump's anti-immigrant policies, which, despite their blatant racism, gained him millions of votes. I remember listening to his voice booming through crowds of MAGA supporters as he ranted about keeping illegal immigrants out of the country with his border wall. It was as blatant as it possibly could be: Trump wanted the United States to become a country that limited the array of identities available to "Americans."

I saw Trump's policies and presidency as having the ability to both distort and destroy the US government's duty to guarantee and uphold the rights of its citizens. And indeed, the ideologies that underpinned his campaign and presidency would, by the end of his administration, shake US democracy to its core. Fast forward to January 6, 2021, and that truly became reality. Trump's trajectory coincided with my immersion into law, politics, and a grassroots movement that aimed to recognize, in Canada, the kind of systemic racism that was on full, horrific display in the United States. This was no coincidence: I felt the urgency to mobilize my community as a counterweight to all that Trump's rise and regime represented and to ensure that it did not land on Canada's shores.

MORE THAN SIX MONTHS after I submitted my application to law school, I had no news. I knew that McGill usually made its first round of admissions in February and that it would be a waiting game after that. Despite a silence well into April, I was still confident I would be admitted. While waiting, I decided to take action to propel my political aspirations. For me, politics wasn't so much about becoming a politician as it was about being the change I wanted to see in the city. Politics would be a way of putting my words into action. Without knowing much about Montreal's political players, I sent an email to the office of the mayor of Montréal-Nord, the city's poorest and arguably most violent district. My goal was to work with youth in the borough and give them the guidance and mentoring that I lacked when growing up. It was important to me to help those in whom I saw myself reflected—the youth of Montréal-Nord who, much like Jugy and me years before, struggled through despair and apathy. I didn't want to see the mistakes I had made be replicated by others, because I knew deep down that without my "guardian angels"— Mom, Dad, Jugy, and Coach Piché—I might be living a vastly different life. Even though I had never lived in Montréal-Nord, I felt deeply connected to the borough and its residents, who, like me, knew what it meant to be alienated and marginalized in society. Montréal-Nord was where inequities lived, so that's where I went.

I was granted a meeting with the borough's mayor, Christine Black. Though she was clearly well-intentioned, it seemed as though issues related to racial profiling, unemployment, health inequity, lack of access to sports centers, and so on were beyond her ken, and her budget. In fairness, the issues I was concerned about were systemic, and no single mayor or other leader could eliminate them. But I felt that I could do more. I could fight for the people. I could give them a voice and be a political leader who would inspire change despite administrative limitations.

To get started, I reached out to local political actors, trying to pave a path into the space. Through a few mutual friends, I met Valérie Plante, a city councilor and leader of the municipal political party Projet Montréal. I viewed Projet Montréal as progressive. It was the only municipal party with a woman at the helm and with policies centered on the environment, social housing, and public transportation.

Valérie and I arranged to meet at a coffee shop downtown. When I arrived, she and her associate, Marie, were already seated. With their exuberant smiles, they greeted me like longtime friends. The more we talked, the more I felt that they were regular Montrealers, like me, who just wanted to make a difference in the city in their own way. Valérie was kind, friendly, and welcoming. I suppose that was her strength; it was what initially attracted me to her team. After that meeting, I decided my political journey, whatever it may be, would start with Projet Montréal.

Although I considered running for political office as an independent, when and if that day came, I saw the opportunity to join an established political party as the best way to address the needs of all Montrealers, particularly vulnerable communities on the periphery of the island.

IN LATE MAY 2017, I finally received word from McGill Law. My heart raced as I opened the email: I had been accepted. The congratulatory words from the admissions committee left me with a mix of shock and exuberance. I knew this was a special moment in my life. I immediately asked a friend, who was equally as shocked as I was, to record my reaction. I wanted to make my intentions clear: "I will support anybody who faces injustice. I will support anybody who faces any kind of obstacle in their life. I'm so happy to have been accepted at McGill Law, and I'm going to give back to everyone around me in the best way that I can. Thank you to everyone who has ever supported me and believed in me."

Although it meant I would be in my first semester of law school while also pursuing political aspirations, the work overload and pressure made me feel alive, and it was a step toward my personal revolution. My involvement in Projet Montréal and now in McGill's law program represented the change that I was striving for. Politics, law school, and academia are highly exclusive, privileged spaces. In fact, McGill not only had roots in the slave trade, as its founder James McGill had been a slave owner, but the institution had also historically limited the number of Black and Jewish students who could attend. In part because of this legacy, I saw my presence on the campus, particularly at the law school, as a triumph. I would be occupying spaces that had historically excluded people who looked like me. As the maxim frequently attributed to Mahatma Gandhi goes, I would be the change I wanted to see in the world.

As the summer drew to a close, and my involvement with Projet Montréal was increasing, it was time to get organized and ready for law school. I knew tackling this new chapter alongside my first political adventure would be challenging, but I was up for it. I thrived and felt alive when I was under pressure.

McGill was largely homogeneous, with few students of color. This gulf was obvious as soon as I stepped foot onto campus for orientation with the rest of the incoming class. But it didn't faze me: I had been on the margins for much of my life, so I was used to it.

I was pleasantly surprised when, in his welcome speech, McGill's dean drew attention to the school's lack of diversity, saying it was a "deficit" he hoped to overcome. It seemed like he and I were on the same page about the need for change, albeit from drastically different perspectives. After a morning of ice-breakers and tours of the school, my first class began. I sat in the middle of the classroom, my eyes glued to the professor, who stood behind a wooden lectern at the front of the room.

"I'd like to begin today's class with a land acknowledgment," she said, slowly and with intention. "McGill University is situated on land which has long served as a site of meeting and exchange amongst Indigenous peoples, including the Haudenosaunee and Anishinaabe nations. We acknowledge and thank the diverse Indigenous peoples whose presence marks this territory on which peoples of the world now gather."

I understood the rationale behind the acknowledgment and appreciated the effort to make students more aware of the legal and social stakes of colonialism, but I wondered why the professor was acknowledging a reality that neither she, nor the institution, nor the province, nor the country itself had any intention to rectify.

I was the first to raise my hand. The professor looked at me, confused, as we had yet to address any material. But that was all the material I needed for my first interjection. "Is McGill going to actively pressure the provincial or federal government to cede the land back to Indigenous groups?" I exclaimed. I wasn't questioning the professor: I was indirectly asking my fellow classmates if we were going to blindly follow the custom. I had heard the same sentiment repeated over and over by folks whose ancestors had colonized the land they were "acknowledging." "Why recognize that we're on unceded territory if there is no intention of giving it back?" I clarified.

The whole class turned toward me, the professor paused, and there was an awkward moment of silence before a fellow student chimed in: "Well, Indigenous peoples have oral traditions, so I think saying it matters."

I looked at her blankly. "Welcome to law school," I thought to myself. No one else said a word, although I'm sure people had thoughts. I didn't understand why they wouldn't speak up. Perhaps it was fear of insulting the professor, or of losing friends on the first day of class. Still, I was surprised. Since we were all law students, I figured my classmates would be just as opinionated and outspoken as I was—that it was basically a prerequisite to becoming a lawyer in the first place. I learned quickly though that some of my class-mates were there to get an education, not to challenge it. This was how we were different. I thought to myself, *Oral traditions don't justify empty words.* I made a concerted effort to shut my mouth, and pick my battles, just like Dad had taught me.

That was my first experience with law: an empty argument to defend a history of genocide and land theft. I decided that si-lence was sometimes better than speaking out, especially in law school.

A FEW MONTHS LATER, a professor in our Legal Foundations course lectured for forty-five minutes about the Thirteenth Amendment to the US Constitution and how it was used to justify modern-day slavery. Although the Thirteenth Amendment formally abolished slavery, its specific language permits slavery and involuntary servitude where they serve as a punishment for a crime. I listened intently to this illustration of how severely the US criminal justice system treats people of color. This form of legalized discrimination is also rampant in US housing, education, employment structures, and public welfare programs. Disenfranchising people of color is a business venture, a goal, and a project of racial domination, albeit one hidden behind the guise of law and order.

For centuries the United States used torture and the intimidation of Black slaves to increase the amount of cotton they could cultivate each day and, in so doing, expand its economy. In other words, innovation in violence served as a foundation of the industrialization of the United States, enslaved people being merely economic tools exploited for private and public gain. Just as slavery is consistently misrepresented as a cultural practice rather than the economic foundation of US expansion into a continental and global power, the modern-day US criminal justice system is misrepresented as a social tool for protection rather than a capitalist venture rooted in the violation of human, civil, and economic rights.

This "prison–business nexus" has revived economically depressed regions of the United States. The Corrections Corporation of America, now called CoreCivic, generated $1.89 billion in the 2016 fiscal year alone—proof that the practice of privatizing prisons in the United States can significantly boost the economy. Prisons are big business and have therefore become deeply entrenched in the US economic and political systems. By increasing the "supply" of prisoners available to them—that is, incarcerating individuals at a higher rate—private prisons expand their potential economic output, leading to an endless cycle of exploitation.

I sat at the front of the class and didn't say a word. I recalled my first interjection on day one of law school and reminded myself that it was best to keep my mouth shut. Motionless like a statue in my seat, I was thinking about inequities in the Canadian justice system, our history of slavery, most notable that we had the first slave, Olivier le Jeune, arrive on our shores in the early 1600s. I knew everyone was waiting for me to address the professor and comment on the content of his lecture. While I sat in silence, my peers had discussions comparing US and Canadian data on issues like racial profiling and incarceration rates. My classmates kept looking in my direction, waiting for me to speak. In fact, my friend and classmate Frank sent me an email during class: "Dude, why aren't you speaking up!!?? This is totally ur TOPIC!"

I responded as soon as I read it. "That's exactly why I'm not speaking. I want to wait and listen to what others have to say."

At long last, what I was waiting for surfaced: the insensitive, ignorant, uncompassionate, white supremacist commentary that often went hand in hand with these types of conversations in these types of settings. But the comment didn't come from just anyone: it fell from the lips of the cohort's top student.

"Well, I think there are benefits to the work being conducted," he said. "These prisoners are learning skills that will assist them in being productive members of society once they're released." I wasn't surprised or shocked. His comment was exactly how privileged white people tended to see Black servitude. Despite being "paid" a few cents per hour, they were "gaining skills." The most concerning part about all this was that these bright minds in these powerful institutions would be the ones running the country.

..

WHILE I WAS IN LAW SCHOOL the provincial government adopted a secularism law known as Bill 21, "an Act respecting the laicity of the State," which prohibits public employees in positions of authority, such as judges, teachers, and police officers, from wearing religious symbols. This law did not come out of nowhere. Quebec had a tumultuous relationship with religion, most notably the Catholic Church. For much of its history, the Catholic Church exercised a tremendous amount of influence over health care, education, social welfare, and Quebec's society at large. With the election of the Liberals of Jean Lesage in 1960, the separation of church and state revved into high gear. The change was so rapid and so widespread that it is often referred to as the "Quiet Revolution" as the state became more secular and separate from the Church. In the name of laicity (secularism), the provincial government imposed this discriminatory law that disproportionately impacted Muslim women, particularly teachers who could no longer work in Quebec because of their religious garments.

The Quebec government was effectively banishing religious minorities and excluding the "other" from Quebec society. This bill sent a clear message to minorities: anyone who does not fit the norm of what it means to be a Quebecer (French and white) should assimilate to the majority or leave. This bill symbolizes, in many ways, a paranoid Quebec that believes that if they, the majority, intermingle with different cultures, their culture will inevitably be weakened and eroded.

The blatantly discriminatory legislation caused an uproar in the city, the province, and the country, to the point that mayors from other Canadian cities began to fund campaigns against Bill 21 and raise money to support legal action against this religious symbol law. Having been raised in an enriching spiritual environment, I never questioned the power and importance of religion as it relates to identity and culture. It is true that religion has led to violence throughout history, but in my life it has provided spiritual solace—a guiding light for individuals and communities alike. But in Quebec, religion (other than Catholicism) was seen as a threat to Quebecer identity and culture. The government of Quebec did not view it as hypocritical to continue to finance churches and maintain the emblematic cross atop Montreal's Mount-Royal, but a Muslim woman with a hijab was somehow a threat to our "secular" society.

Bill 21 caused massive daily protests, and I attended as many as I could, marching alongside activists shouting "Liberté! Égalité!" But though their fervor was inspiring, I knew in my heart that the protests would be fruitless: religious minorities in the province had virtually no power in the face of a government primarily composed of white francophones who saw multiculturalism and religious diversity as a threat. Moreover, the government used a notwithstanding clause in the Canadian Constitution to protect the law from being struck down in the courts. Legally and politically, this felt like checkmate.

The furor reminded me of what Timothy Snyder had written in his book *On Tyranny* about the Nazis in twentieth-century Germany—namely, that people shouldn't take it for granted that institutions will always "preserve decency." William Steinberg, mayor of Hampstead, made similar connections when he suggested that the Quebec government was leaning toward "ethnic cleansing" by legislating this ban on religious symbols.

While the dissenting voices that considered Bill 21 a means of ethnic cleansing were met with criticism, one thing was certain: Quebecers and Canadians at large could not take the Canadian Constitution for granted. While religious liberties, gender rights, and racial and language rights could be prescribed, there was no guarantee that they would be respected, protected, and fulfilled by our institutions.

Thinking back to my time in Boisbriand, I realized that with Bill 21 the Quebec government wanted to frame a particular profile. If people didn't fit the mythical norm of what it meant to be a Quebecer—that is, French and white—they would be greeted with suspicion and deemed threatening to French language and culture. Quebec's premier, François Legault, who had the benefit of a majority Coalition Avenir Québec government, kept pounding his chest to emphasize that the secularism law reflected the will of the majority of Quebecers. It didn't matter to him that his "tyranny-of-the-majority" ideology infringed on the rights of minorities and circumvented the Quebec and Canadian Charters of Rights and Freedoms, which are supposed to protect the minority from the will and whim of the majority. I saw Bill 21 not just as an attempt to homogenize Quebec, but as yet another way the province was putting up more walls to exclude *itself* from the world stage. The barriers had been set, and I wanted to tear them down.

In a democracy where citizens are engaged, when some of us have our rights infringed upon, we all have our rights infringed upon. With my legal education in progress, I felt a sense of power and responsibility to fight this and any other law or policy that divided my home city of Montreal.

ELEVEN

POLITICAL MOVES

Throughout my first term at McGill Law, I remained committed to Projet Montréal, attending meetings with my team, rallies, and community events. I was dedicated to growing the party for the upcoming 2017 municipal election, in which I would now be a candidate. It would be my first time running a campaign. I knew that being in the public eye as a political hopeful would be pressure—not only for me, but for our lead mayoral candidate, Valérie Plante. As the first woman leading the party, she faced gender bias and harassment, and I wanted to be there for her. We felt like a team.

Valérie offered me the position of her co-lister, the equivalent of the vice president on the ballot. Not only would she place me in a borough that I could easily win, but I would be guaranteed a seat on the party's executive committee, and the handsome six-figure salary that went along with it. It seemed like an ideal opportunity. Once elected to office, I could work to push the city council's political agenda toward a more equitable and inclusive Montreal.

But I knew deep down that her offer wasn't the right move for me. Although it would allow me to achieve my political goals without much friction, my mission went beyond financial and political gain. Dad used to tell me, "Don't let financial insecurity influence your actions and undermine your integrity." Guided by the swamis' daily teachings, I always knew right from wrong, good from evil. Yes, teenage angst and the social obstacles I faced in Montreal had led me astray, but my strong roots and moral compass had eventually prevailed. Now I needed to follow that moral compass; I was sure it would guide me in the right direction.

So, I decided to run for mayor of Montréal-Nord against the incumbent, Christine Black, whom I had met with the previous year. As a low-income borough that was home to new immigrants and families, Montréal-Nord reflected my upbringing and my struggles. It was where change was needed most. Montréal-Nord also has its share of wealthy residents, who live in massive homes along the water in the borough's northern coast. In this, Montréal-Nord is a microcosm of the inequality gap.

But my affinity for the borough and its residents was not always mutual. Residents were proud of their borough despite its challenges, especially members of the local Haitian community, which is one of Canada's largest. Some of the Haitian leaders and top activists looked at me—an Anglo-Jamaican from the south of Montreal—as an outsider. It made no difference that my French was now fluent. All my life I'd been too white to fit in with the Black folks and too Black to fit in with the white folks. Empowered by life experiences, I balked at the idea that my color, light skin and all, language, and location in the city should override my pursuits of social justice. Barack Obama, similarly, had gone to the South Side of Chicago as a community organizer with good intentions, but folks saw him as being out of place. That didn't dissuade him, however. I had experienced marginality and exclusion because of my skin color and language, but I overcame the internal demons that told me to hide, freeze, and escape because I was too different.

Also, the dynamic of being from the south of Montreal versus the north felt petty and irrelevant. I had just traveled the world, living thousands of miles away in China, Egypt, and Dubai, so I scoffed at the narrow view that I had less credibility because my own doorstep was a few miles away from the borough.

But my logic was not accepted by the community hierarchy. Who was I to run there? Without backing down, I went on local talk radio shows and challenged my critics: "I'll step down right now if you step up! Who else is gonna step up?" Then I'd start barking out names of top figures in the Montréal-Nord community—folks who criticized me privately, saluted me publicly, and shied away from running in the election themselves. With no takers, it was up to me to run an election in the hood and expose the injustices that were being ignored by the current administration. This is politics though, not activism—the challenges that I was about to face were enormous.

Poverty, exclusion, and disenfranchisement had multiple consequences for the borough, including low voter turnout. Who was in power tended to be decided by a minority of older voters, many of whom lived in the big houses along the water and in senior homes along the river side; these were folks who were courted and influenced by the same *friendly* politicians and, as a result, were entrenched in their voting habits. The same politicians kept getting reelected. In fact, the party of Denis Coderre governed the city, including the borough of Montréal-Nord. As a lifelong politician and former minister of immigration, Coderre was a force to be reckoned with, at least in Montréal-Nord. I had as much chance of winning there as a Democrat in rural Texas.

For what felt like weeks, I contemplated whether to run in

Montréal-Nord or to take the easier route to a win in downtown Montreal. I consulted with friends and family. Representing one of Montreal's poorest boroughs would be more fulfilling because it was where I could potentially enact the most change. I felt, from the moment I stepped foot in the borough, that I could be the voice its residents needed. I truly believed that I understood them and their community's needs on a deeper level than their current elected officials. I had lived their lives. I had walked in their shoes.

My intuition was lively, my instincts sharp, a gift I got from my mother. She often told me to follow my heart, especially in moments of indecision when my heart and mind were disconnected: my mind was invoking political wins and financial gain, but my heart was directing me to stand up for my rights, for our rights. "Listen to your heart and follow your intuition," she would say to me, poetically, in her thick French accent. It was in moments like these that I wished, even more than usual, that she were here. I knew my judgment, like hers, was based on a mix of instinct and spirituality. If I listened to my heart, I could not lose. My heart was connected to the moral universe, and if I followed it, even a political loss would fade over time if I was on the right side of history. I believed what Martin Luther King Jr. said, that the arc of the moral universe is long, but bends toward justice. It wasn't about the quick win, but rather the long-term vision to reshape society.

My heart directed me to Montréal-Nord, to use my voice there to advance public dialogue about key issues related to education, economic inequality, sports and recreation infrastructure, and youth engagement and representation in the city. I wanted to focus on the bigger picture: molding the next generation of youth to take hold of their futures and command of their lives. I recalled the apathetic high-school dropout I had been, lying on Dad's sofa. All it took was a person who looked like me—that five-foot-eleven, 180-pound NFL defensive back I watched on a Sunday long ago—to ignite a flame in me and get me back on-track. Now it was my turn to give back, to be the role model that could spark change in the next generation. I might not be able to implement all the changes I wanted in the borough, but as a young Black man running for mayor of Montréal-Nord, I could inspire the next generation—racialized boys and girls who didn't see themselves reflected at any level of government—to be that change. That, for me, would be a victory. I aspired to diversify representation in local government. Without representation, there is no recognition of the minority's problems, economic, social, or otherwise; and without recognition, there can be no equitable redistribution of resources. As we approach the end of the first quarter of the twenty-first century, Montréal-Nord, a borough with a population of more than eighty thousand, remains without a sports center. That injustice alone made me want to fight for change in this underserved borough of seemingly undeserving youth.

I wanted to give those youth hope that, despite their social circumstances, they could make something of their lives, that they could thrive and govern their neighborhoods according to their own interests. They didn't have to fall into the dangerous trap of poverty and violence. They could make a difference—for themselves, their communities, and the world. And so I turned away from the money and political guarantees and chose the political lion's den: Montréal-Nord.

WITH A FULL COURSE load at McGill Law and a campaign for mayor of Montréal-Nord happening at the same time, I was in the eye of the storm. My life was like an action movie. The sense of adventure, risk, and pressure was a rush. My campaign was unconventional. Lacking time to do the tried-and-true knocking-on-doors method to connect with voters, I visited community organizations, restaurants, schools, and barbershops and hooped with local youth.

Midafternoon in Montréal-Nord, I stopped at a local high school to meet teachers and students, to share my vision for the borough. At the sight of the outdoor basketball court, unable to resist the urge to play a game of pick-up, I challenged the top baller on the court. After getting scored on, I decided to get in the game, and hype myself up. I squatted down in a defensive stance, slapped the pavement with my hands, and ripped my pants from my belt line down my rear to the leg of my pants. The cries of laughter and awe blasted through the court. I hid my embarrassment and continued to play, undeterred, as the students cheered and yelled, "Oh, il naise pas le gars" ("Oh, this guy ain't playin'"). Connecting with the next generation and bringing the issues to light were more important to me than winning an election. My determination, honesty, and authenticity became clearer the more I visited the borough. My ground game and presence in the community were also starting to earn me the respect of my earlier critics. I was earning my stripes.

WHEN YOU'RE BALANCING WORK as a political candidate with a divided family unit, there are no fairy tales, just raw reality. As I was racing to class one day, I got a call from Dad.

"They evicted me," he calmly said.

"What? Evicted you? How is that possible?" I asked in shock. He told me he had been meditating under a tree next to Saint Joseph's Oratory, Montreal's grandest religious institution, for the past three days. He had finally mustered up the courage to call me. But he was calm. Almost too calm. For my dad, this was karma, life forces beyond his control. It was all part of God's plan.

I didn't know it, but the Quebec government had been warning Dad about a possible eviction, holding multiple court hearings for years under the premise that his apartment was a fire hazard. He never asked me for help and never said a word about it. The province had now successfully evicted him. I was upset, but not surprised by the way the "justice" system had dealt with him. Quebec has a poor record on mental health and homelessness, and that, coupled with my dad's marginalization, led to complete social banishment. To make things worse, the government was evicting him a couple of months before Quebec's brutal winter, leaving him barely enough time to find a new place to live. They had set a dumpster below his balcony and tossed out all his pos-sessions. The judge, the housing bureau, the city, the opposition lawyer—the entire system—had worked against this sixty-nine-year-old man, heartlessly condemning him to homelessness.

Dad, though, viewed his situation as an act of God. In the Hindu tradition, accumulating material possessions is frowned upon, and now God had taken all his possessions except his wallet and the clothes on his back. He lost many of my belongings too: my uni-versity and CFL football jerseys, the Bol d'Or championship ring, and, more importantly, my library. And yet instead of holding the officials who put him in this situation in contempt, my dad simply told them they would have to face God one day. He was always direct yet gracious in the face of adversity. The material loss was, in his eyes, a spiritual gain.

A few weeks after his eviction, my dad decided to move to the temple that he and Mom had attended when they were younger.

Since he was a deeply spiritual man, the temple's parishioners had offered him refuge. This gave Dad peace. The temple was where he was meant to be, and he felt that God, however tumultuously, had guided him there.

DESPITE MY FAMILY STRUGGLES, I had to keep moving forward. Back on the campaign trail I got energy from my team, especially from Mathieu Léonard, a candidate running for councilor in my district. Mathieu had taken a journey similar to mine, having dropped out of high school and then finding his way to boxing through a local organization called Ali et les Princes de la rue. Given his background and life experiences, he could relate to my mission. We knew we were fighting against an institutional behemoth in Denis Coderre, but like me, Mathieu would never back down from a fight. By running in Montréal-Nord, we had effectively eliminated ourselves from mainstream media attention, so I began to focus on social media. Despite being on the margins, I could circumvent the media and get my message across to my audience. My opponents were relatively silent, nowhere to be found, on social media or otherwise. They had a political stronghold. The more they hid and stayed quiet, the better their chances of winning.

IT WAS COLD AND RAINY on the morning of election day, November 5, 2017. As people lined up to vote, I toured the polling stations with my team, greeting voters as they exited. In the distance we saw what seemed to be hundreds of people leaving a church. When we scurried over to encourage them to vote, our enthusiasm was met with a "why vote, nothing will ever change" attitude.

For these churchgoers, praying to God seemed like a more real-istic way to enact change than voting for a politician. After all, God was more trustworthy than politicians, who had a habit of coming to the neighborhood during the election with promises, and disappearing once elected. It was the classic, overpromise and under-deliver that they had seen before. Historically speaking, I suppose they were right. In this low-income borough, things change, but often for the worse. With all the issues of crime, un-employment, unsanitary housing, and much more, the citizens of Montréal-Nord seemed hopeless during the election. After hours of touring stations and talking to people, I felt a strong sense that our party leader, Valérie Plante, would pull it off, but I was con-cerned that nothing would change, just like those churchgoers had prophesized. Looking back now, they were right.

As the day came to an end, I began the thirty-minute drive home from Montréal-Nord to my apartment in the city's down-town core. Law school, the election, the turmoil with Dad, and a series of personal ups and downs had taken an emotional toll on me. I hadn't cried in years, but during that car ride home, tears ran down my face, blurring my vision. I felt a mix of pride, happiness, and emotional and mental exhaustion. I had entered a political lion's den when I chose to run in Montréal-Nord, and that was a challenge I embraced. But just because I had grit and determina-tion didn't mean that it wasn't mentally, physically, and emotion-ally draining. On a pursuit to raise awareness about issues that were central to improving the lives of those on the margin, I felt as though my team and I accomplished our mission.

During the campaign, I knew we had made a difference for at least some of the borough's residents. Regardless of the vote count, win or lose, I was proud of the work we did.

..

As IT TURNED OUT, unsurprisingly, I lost the election in my district. And yet, as the rest of the results were announced, and Valérie Plante became the first female mayor in Montreal's history, I felt elated and joyful. We'd been successful in getting people who had never voted before out to the polls. We engaged youth. We showed unparalleled dedication to the city. We sacrificed for the greater good. And we set the foundation for what felt like a new political movement in Montreal.

It was momentous, and we were ecstatic: for Valérie, for women, and for what seemed to be a new path toward greater representation in the municipal government. It was clear from the beginning of the campaign that, to have a chance of winning, Valérie would need to overcome a series of gendered obstacles and systemic biases entrenched in Montreal's political system. But she did. We did.

I was particularly happy for her because, despite my own loss, the party would now be moving in the right direction. If our victory had a thorn, it was that the party did not elect a single visible minority within city council members. But I still had confidence that Valérie Plante would be an effective leader, work across party lines, address economic inequality and housing issues, and the like. I believed she would redefine the city's political priorities by bringing in a diverse team of people to provide a new perspective on mainstream political issues.

Based on the relationship I developed with our new mayor during the campaign, I assumed that I, as a community liaison, would now be able to get items on the political agenda that reflected the real needs of Montrealers. Items that addressed diversity, inclusion, and, most importantly, the next generation in a meaningful way.

..

A DAY AFTER THE ELECTION, I was scheduled to speak with Mike Finnerty on CBC Radio's Montreal morning show *Daybreak*. Despite my loss, I was energized and ready to make a change with the help of our new administration and mayor. It felt like my party had taken down the establishment. I was on cloud nine.

"Balarama!" Valérie shouted when she saw me in the lobby of the studio. We walked toward each other and exchanged a big hug.

"We did it!" I rumbled, in my 5:30 a.m. voice.

"Oh my god, I still can't believe it!" she replied. "I can't wait to get things moving!"

"Yes, let's talk soon!" I said, already planning how I could help address social and economic issues in the city.

The election was over, but I was still in game mode. When I took my seat in the interview booth, I knew what was about to come my way. The mayor's victory was tainted with exclusion; of the sixty-five councilors elected, only four were people of color, and all of them with the opposition.

Mike avoided softball questions and immediately got to the point. "Is this what systemic racism looks like?" he asked. "No one is saying Projet Montréal was malicious or was being discriminatory in their intent, but the system in place has produced white rule."

I paused to consider whether my response should be political or from the heart. I decided to follow my heart and speak my truth, as I had always done.

"When we look at the political system today, we can trace it back to a political, racial, hierarchy system of 375 years ago [when Montreal was founded]. Yes, systemic racism is embedded in our laws and our institutions, and our goal is to reform that," I said.

I entered politics to change the system, but it turned out that the system was on autopilot, reproducing the same inequities with every passing election. With sixty-five city council members, Montreal has the largest municipal council in North America (compared with Toronto's twenty-six and New York City's fifty-one). The majority of them, knowingly or unknowingly, reproduce inequality and discrimination with silence and inaction.

THE MAYOR WAS INAUGURATED the following week, but I, and all the other "losing" candidates, weren't invited to the event. Members of Valérie Plante's cabinet chalked this up to "protocol," suggesting it wasn't standard practice to allow unsuccessful candidates to attend. But a glance at the invited group made it obvious: people of color were excluded from the inauguration—because all people of color in the party had lost.

I texted James, a member of the mayor's cabinet, to let him know I thought the mayor was wrong for not inviting us to the inauguration.

He responded bureaucratically that there weren't enough seats for everyone. I was on the outs, and I knew it.

When I asked about being appointed as a liaison between the party and cultural communities, James replied, essentially, that I should send my résumé. And that was it.

In my mind, the relationship was severed. To add insult to injury, I received a call the very next day asking me to donate to the party. Call it politics if you want, but to me, it was Exploitation 101. Valérie Plante had won, in part off the backs of candidates of color, and now she wanted us to pay her for it, literally.

My intuition told me all I needed to know—that the mayor had used people of color for political gain. In retrospect, there had been some red flags during the campaign, including lack of financial resources and support for candidates of color, but I hadn't thought much of it. I rationalized the uneven distribution of resources as a political move to prioritize candidates who were most likely to win.

I recognized that, for the party, winning was the only objective. But the candidates who received the most support from the party were also overwhelmingly white and francophone. In fact, when the mayor announced her Executive Committee a few days later, not a single person of color was selected to work in her "inner circle," despite the campaign being centered on diversity and inclusion. It was as if she didn't see the irony: that this was an overt embodiment of systemic racism. At the time, 33 percent of Montreal's population identified as a visible minority, so having no representation in government was a slap in the face, especially to all of the candidates of color who worked so hard to get the mayor elected under the promise that things would change. But the election was over now. To the new administration, we were clearly expendable. The disrespect was inspiring, it was fuel to tackle not just a fragile city council but systemic racism and discrimination throughout the city of Montreal.

WITH THE TURBULENCE OF THE ELECTION OVER, I needed to refocus my energy on law school. I spent most of my time in the library, studying to catch up on the work I had missed while campaigning. One day, while taking a break from tort law readings, I was scrolling through my Facebook feed catching up on the news when I came across an article that began with the following line: "Quebec's legislature has passed a motion calling on store clerks to stick with a simple 'bonjour' when greeting customers instead of the 'bonjour-hi' often heard in Montreal."

I couldn't believe what I was reading. The government wanted to bar store clerks from greeting people with "hi" as a way to protect the French language. It reminded me of all my years in grade school and high school, being policed by teachers and administrators to not speak English in the hallways. The subsequent adoption of the "Bonjour-Hi motion" by all political parties in Quebec made it abundantly clear that none of them could claim to represent multi-cultural communities and linguistic minorities in the province. Although the motion may have seemed trivial to people outside of Quebec, and even throughout Canada for that matter, it served to reexacerbate linguistic tensions in the province by reinforcing petty language motions with no legal teeth on those who didn't speak French, or were still learning to. Instead of promoting French, already the province's official language, the legislature was targeting the word "hi" as if eliminating its use would somehow improve or strengthen French language and culture in Quebec. In 2020, the Bloc Québécois party launched a campaign to encourage businesses to greet people with "Bonjour-Ho" at Christmastime, until, that is, the ridicule grew too great and the party quietly retracted it. Whether it was "Hi" or "Ho," the government was heading in the wrong direction.

I sat back in my chair, staring aimlessly at the green lamp casting its glow over my laptop screen. My mind was numb, but I was also shocked and frustrated. I'd had enough. I thought back to my motivation for attending law school in the first place. I'd wanted to change my city, to make it a place that everyone could call home.

Forgetting about my approaching exams, I immediately began looking into how I could legally force a conversation on systemic racism and discrimination. The system was looking to fight, and I was ready to scrap. The politicians in power were too white, too blind, too passive to take action. I came across the Montreal Charter of Rights and Responsibilities and began to assess what legally binding obligations the municipality had in relation to minorities. A participatory democracy clause in Article 16 (h) noted that any citizen who collected fifteen thousand signatures on a given matter could legally oblige the city to hold a public consultation within municipal jurisdiction. I'd found my legal tool, and I was about to use it on a homogeneous City Hall and Executive Committee.

I grabbed my phone and jumped up from my chair as I typed out a post on social media: "I am going to launch a legally binding petition enshrined in the participatory democracy clause in the Montreal Charter of Rights and Responsibilities to force the City of Montreal to hold a public consultation on systemic racism and discrimination." My aim was not just to confront City Hall, but to tackle employment, housing, racial profiling, urban planning and territorial disparities, culture, and the lack of sports infrastructure in low-income neighborhoods throughout the city. It was a "go-big-or-go-home" approach, but it was necessary. I was on a mission to launch the city's biggest advocacy campaign on systemic racism.

My post struck a chord with the media throughout Montreal—a city that had clearly been turning a blind eye to systemic racism and inequality. Like the cold showers I used to take each morning in the ashram, I had doused city council, media, and anyone who cared to read with the cold hard truth. My rapidly expanding knowledge of the law, and, more important, the critical skills my legal education was giving me, would provide me with the power to influence Montreal's governance structures. The post was another step toward me becoming the social and legal architect that could redesign our city.

The media was in a frenzy, the public onlookers surprised. There was also panic, particularly in political circles. But despite the uproar, the mayor strategically remained quiet. But it did not matter. My activism was going beyond local politics now. I was fighting, on a grassroots level, against systemic racism, and for equality and sociopolitical justice.

The provincial government had long declined to hold such inquiries, and the City of Montreal had refused to recognize the systemic nature of racism or discrimination. These were deep-seated issues that required radical action if change was to come about. To this day, the premier of Quebec denies the existence of systemic racism, racial profiling, and maltreatment of minorities and Indigenous people in hospitals in the province. Compounded by a lack of understanding of intersectionality and other key equity issues, the provincial government seems stuck in the past. I was trying to bring it into the future.

In addition to these setbacks, the thorns of my biracialism also started to arise, again. Members of the Black community saw me as a cocky upstart who wasn't Black enough to represent Black interests, while white people saw me as a sore loser who was merely unhappy with the election results. Not fitting squarely into either of these racial groups, I didn't care. I was doing my best to advance a dialogue based on equity, justice, and fairness, but for most people, it seemed like this wasn't enough. Despite dedicating my time and energy to the cause, showing up for my community when I needed to, I was seen as an outcast solely because of my identity. At this point, though, I was used to "marching to the beat of my own drum," so overcoming the odds and being shunned by a community I identified with didn't faze me. If anything, I viewed it as a flaw in their logic. Why, as a Black man, should I not be allowed to represent Black interests? Why should I not be allowed to advocate for Black rights in a city where I had faced the harsh realities of racism and discrimination from the day I arrived? It made little sense to me. So I kept pushing. I kept making my voice heard. Because I knew that what I was doing was the right thing. I knew I was on the right side of history.

As when I ran for mayor of Montréal-Nord, I wouldn't always have institutions and community leaders on my side. But I had something more important: the people. The many messages of support I received confirmed that I was making the right call. The more I challenged the system, the more those in its upper echelons criticized me, and the more regular people stood behind me. It was the beginning of a true grassroots movement.

TWELVE

THE PETITION: A COLLECTION OF ASPIRATIONS

I had entered the political arena full of optimism, ready to break down the rigid pillars of unjust institutions. Instead, I got politically crushed and racially tokenized. I remained, however, committed to my mission to dissolve societal divisions and build a community in Montreal where everyone felt at home.

I was now thirty-four years old and understood that the more life experience I gained, the more empowered I felt. Despite the many challenges I'd faced, my faith in the world and in myself had never faded. Things had been hard at times, but I'd never become jaded. With the energy of the wild country boy I was at heart, I was ready to take on the city, not as a politician, but as a fiery activist.

Activism requires a unique set of skills and leadership style. Some of this came naturally to me, other elements I had to actively cultivate. Community activism also revealed what felt like a personal paradox. I knew, from my world travels and the sense of community I'd had during my childhood at the ashram, that a collective approach would be key to successful activism, even though, instinctually, I was fiercely independent. Perhaps this had to do with my growing up without a stable parental situation at home. Although the swamis and my guardians had supported me, I'd constantly felt like I was in survival mode. I knew I had to fend for myself.

My athletic life had also contributed to this independent spirit. Despite playing professional football—one of the ultimate team sports—deep down I preferred track because it was all up to me. But that's how I thrived: with the pressure on my shoulders, and my shoulders alone.

Activism, however, is not an individual game; it's a collective team effort that requires community, cooperation, and collaboration with allies *and* opponents. If I was going to fulfill, uphold, and protect our collective rights, I needed to limit my penchant for individuality. In the arena of community development, I knew that my ability to mobilize people from all walks of life would determine my success or failure. After all, one person with a pen and pad could not conceivably collect fifteen thousand handwritten signatures in the ninety-day window cribbed in the law.

FOLLOWING MY ANNOUNCEMENT ABOUT launching a legally binding petition on systemic racism and discrimination, I reached out to the city's top organizations, including the Côte-des-Neiges Black Community Association led by Tiffany Callender. Tiffany was not only an executive and a mother, but a role model and mentor for members of the Black community. She was a fierce and inspiring leader. She guided me through the politics of community organizing and helped me expand my reach. At the same time, her prowess as a leader forced me to acknowledge a simple yet telling reality: Montrealers, myself included, were so enthralled with the idea of a woman being mayor that few considered how her white privilege—coupled with her francophone identity—allowed her to effectively navigate the political system to gain power. The same couldn't be said for Black women. After the 2017 election, feminism was all the buzz in Montreal, but many of those claiming to be feminists turned a blind eye toward intersectionality and thus systemic racism.

In my view, Tiffany was as qualified as the mayor to govern Montreal, if not more so. Just as my identity had been a liability throughout my life, particularly in all-white spaces, so it was for Black women across the world. Hearing Tiffany's story, and those of so many other women of color, I knew that the city couldn't advance toward justice and fairness while ignoring the realities of intersectionality. The ease with which white women leverage feminism (intentionally or unintentionally) to gain power speaks not just to the existence of systemic racism, but also to the need to address its intersectional character, that is, the complex matrix of advantage and disadvantage in which various elements of identity (race, gender, class, sexual orientation, [dis]ability, religion, language, etc.) overlap and diverge.

THANKS TO TIFFANY'S GUIDANCE, momentum for the petition grew. We announced it, and our partnerships, in 2018 on February 11, the day Nelson Mandela was released from prison in 1990, at Union United Church—Mandela having visited the church on his 1990 visit to the city. Organizations from across Montreal came out in droves to support our initiative.

Situated in Montreal's Little Burgundy neighborhood, Union

United, Canada's oldest Black church, is unassuming and humble. In 1907, Black railway porters and their wives established the non-denominational congregation and moved to the greystone church in 1917. It became a catalyst for social movements focused on equality and justice. Union United's energy and symbolism were empowering. Historically, the church was strengthened by the leadership of Black women, many from the Coloured Women's Club of Montreal, Canada's oldest Black women's institution, advocating for gender *and* racial equality. For years, the church had also played a central role in developing social welfare policies to advance equality for all. It was a beacon for civil rights and Black empowerment in Canada. It was here, at the community and grassroots level, that change sprouted. We were standing on the shoulders of giants, carrying on a long legacy of revolution.

There was an effervescent spirit in the air as we gathered in the church basement, which had quickly filled with community activists, organization executives, churchgoers, and politicians from all the major municipal parties. Looking at all the faces in the room, I was filled with hope. Despite our differences, we were a community. We all had our stories and our struggles, which our individuality may have helped us survive. Now we were coming together to thrive, grow, and build. As the proverb goes: *If you want to go fast, go alone; if you want to go far, go together.*

For two months following the February 11 event, I worked day in and day out to solidify support for the petition. With Tiffany's help, Montreal in Action, the nonprofit I had envisioned establishing in 2016, had finally come into being. We held community meetings, discussed partnerships with leading advocacy organizations, and established a core team of supporters who would work to promote the petition in their social circles. I began to lobby city councilors to present a motion at City Hall on the public consultation: the mayor and the Executive Committee had the power to mandate the Office de consultation publique de Montréal (OCPM) to hold one without the necessity of collecting fifteen thousand signatures. But the councilors never presented the motion, and the mayor indicated that she would "let us do" our work and collect the signatures.

I was not surprised by the mayor's and city councilors' inaction. Racism lives and breathes in silence especially in Canada. Rights won't wait for complacent politicians; rights are achieved when we fight for them. Their inaction, however, was a blessing in disguise. Community organizations had the opportunity to participate in our democracy by engaging with the city's residents to advance our cause and raise awareness about racism and discrimination. Simply put: political inaction and apathy were the fertilizer of our grassroots movement.

On May 1, 2018, International Workers' Day, I set off with a stack of clipboards, boxes of pens, and a motivated team composed of Montreal in Action volunteers and representatives from a variety of community organizations. Our goal was to collect the signatures by July 29, the city's deadline. Now that the petition was public knowledge, I was seen as a radical, particularly by white francophones. Relishing their criticism and skepticism, I was happy to assume the label they imposed upon me. I was okay with being a "radical" especially if it meant that I was fighting against racism and their rigid, discriminatory systems. The hate was fuel for inspiration.

In the first month, our volunteers worked with student unions and community organizations to canvas every corner of Montreal, from parks to mosques to arenas and festivals. We worked tirelessly, even in the early days of a heat wave that ravaged the city and killed more than sixty people over the course of a few weeks. But the heat wave, coupled with the limited resources of the community organizations that had joined with us to launch the petition, eventually took its toll, and many of the volunteers fell off the bandwagon. We were lagging behind on our signature targets, and the clock was ticking. Tiffany and I had to pivot our strategy.

I had personally been paying for all our supplies. But with the petition in flux, and my income during law school next to nothing, a personal line of credit became my only option to fund the operation. The only money I had to my name had come from gigs on diversity panels and a part-time managerial job at a commercial building on Saint-Laurent Boulevard, one of Montreal's liveliest streets and a traditional destination for the waves of immigrants that had come to the city over the decades.

In early June, a month after the petition had been launched, I was locking up when I saw a young man with paint splattered across his clothes peering into the building's front window.

"Hey, you need anything?" I asked.

"Yeah, actually. I would love to rent this space for Mural, a big upcoming arts festival. But I've been negotiating with the building's agent without any luck," he told me.

After a brief conversation, including his telling me a bit about himself—his name was Oliver, and he had been a street artist for years—I decided to help him out. The space was a dream for an artist like him, but it was well beyond his budget. I told him I thought I could broker a deal with the owner, at least for the summer months, and sure enough, in fewer than twenty-four hours, I had secured a significant discount for Oliver, who, unbeknownst to me, was one of the city's top artists. In a matter of weeks, the space became not only a gallery for his work, but a home for other artists from around the city. On top of that, we came to an agreement whereby I could also use the space to collect signatures. It was a win-win.

Each day, I would leave my apartment at the crack of dawn to canvas the city with Montreal in Action volunteers. In the afternoons, I set up shop at the front of the gallery to collect signatures from those lured in by the wild contemporary sculptures and paintings on display there. The gallery also attracted a stream of artistic revolutionaries, break-dancers, and DJs. As we amassed signatures, I thought more about the relationship between art and activism. In time, I would come to think of Oliver's work and his murals throughout the city—and murals in general—as a metaphor for what we were doing as we collected signatures in the gallery and on the streets: together, we were using our common vision and revolutionary spirit to create what amounted to a collective, endlessly layered painting. The sense of creativity, cross-fertilization, and infinite possibility of those days was thrilling.

A light-skinned, stocky DJ from New York named Abdou who was studying business at McGill and hanging out at the gallery was particularly interested in what I was doing. Always on the hunt for an opportunity, and having lived in both New York and Montreal, Abdou had a clear-eyed perspective on things: "Y'all don't need the States to talk about racism; people be racist as f*ck here." A newcomer to the city—and the country—Abdou didn't need a Canadian history lesson to understand that Canada, like the United States, had its own battles with historic and contemporary racism and discrimination.

Abdou was an entrepreneur, but at heart he was a revolutionary. I sold him on the idea of partnering to support my cause. Eager to hop on board, Abdou got his promotional events company, KAJ Collective, to support the petition. He even put together a small team he called "Team No Sleep" to help me collect the remaining signatures. And that's when the game changed. Team No Sleep were not just volunteers; they had a mandate and funding from my line of credit to collect the signatures we needed. Through a combination of business sense and street smarts, we got the petition back in operation. With my dedicated team of volunteers from Montreal in Action as a base and Team No Sleep supporting us, we were unstoppable. We capitalized on large crowds and curious minds across the island. Each day, we verified and counted each signature and began to stack our paper mountain.

We were still in the process of collecting signatures in June when I met Darnella. A half-Jamaican, half-Italian beauty, she was walking down the street with her friend when I called her over to sign. Dressed simply in a white shirt and loose summer pants, with her hair in a bun, she immediately grabbed my attention. After a brief conversation about the petition, I mustered the courage to ask whether she had an Instagram account. She smiled, took my phone, and tapped "follow" on her account. "This is it," I whispered to my friend Prince, who was nearby. With a strong sense that this was a turning point in my life, the start of something special, I asked him to snap a few pictures of me and Darnella.

On our first date, I took Darnella to Jean-XXIII, my old high school in Dorval, to shoot some hoops. Afterward, we strolled the boardwalk along the St. Lawrence River, where I used to hang out with my friends. Instead of taking her on a typical first-date dinner, I wanted to show her my little world. After that, whenever I wasn't collecting signatures, I was with her. It was like high-school love all over again.

ON JULY 27, 2018, two days before our deadline, I brought together members of Montreal in Action and Team No Sleep to formally deposit the twenty-two thousand signatures we had collected—seven thousand more than I had expected. Once we got the ball rolling and people saw that the goal of fifteen thousand signatures was possible, more and more volunteers showed up at our locations. As a result, we wildly surpassed our goal. I was incredibly proud of the work we had done and the petition's reach throughout the city.

With the warm July sun beaming down on us, we marched to City Hall, twenty-two in our group, each carrying one thousand signatures in their hands. No elected official or institution could stop us now. Stack by stack, we piled the signatures on the clerk's desk. In the months leading up to this moment, we had become a group of revolutionaries. And we were about to make history by demanding that the municipal government recognize what it had long denied: that systemic racism in Montreal was real and it needed to be addressed.

As the cameras clicked and rolled, all the attention was directed toward me. During the collection of signatures, I had been, for the first time in my life, not just a community member, but a clear leader. And it made me reflect on the leaders who had guided me in the past. The ashram had had a level of hierarchy that, as a child, I'd been unaware of. The swamis had the nicest sandalwood perfume, wore the most beautiful saffron silk dhotis, and ate the most opulent meals. But if they were so connected to God, why did they feel the need to embrace that elitism? Spiritual leaders—swamis, priests, imams—inhabited hierarchies similar to those of the political leaders I had encountered. Depositing those signatures, I wanted to present a different kind of leadership to those in attendance, one that repudiated hierarchy. From the beginning of the petition—and in all of my work—I had aimed to democratize the team as much as possible.

At the beginning of the media scrum, I had an opportunity to make this ethos especially clear. I turned toward the cameras and the microphones. "Your headline should be, '50 Youth Community Leaders Force a Public Consultation on Systemic Racism,' not 'Balarama Holness,' because I got about 3 percent; 97 percent is from the people in this room. That should be your headline!"

I continued with the basis for our petition, "We are bridging the gap between the streets of Montreal and a *homogeneous* City Hall—a City Hall that does not represent Montrealers. We got twenty-two thousand signatures, and are where we are today, thanks to the dynamic leaders who came out from their respective communities. So, let's make no mistake about it: it's because of these people, each of them with about one thousand signatures in their hands, that Montreal and Quebec are moving toward equality."

It would prove a catalyst for the City of Montreal to finally address systemic racism. With the signatures approved, the Executive Committee was legally obligated to mandate that the OCPM hold a consultation on systemic racism and discrimination. The consultation would be headed by Dominique Ollivier, a Haitian woman with a proven track record in politics, management, and governance. I was confident the consultation would make an important difference in the lives of many in the community—not just of the racialized, but of those who faced injustice and marginalization or who simply struggled to have their voices heard.

WITH THE SIGNATURE COLLECTION OVER, I was back to focusing on school and nurturing my new relationship with Darnella. This was especially important to me because, for years, I had wanted a family of my own. During my public speeches, even in my McGill

Law acceptance video, I always referred to my future children and the impact I wanted to have on their lives and that of the next generation. Just as I aimed to alchemize hate, racism, and silence into openness, hope, and dialogue, so too did I long to overcome the challenges of my childhood by creating a tight-knit family of my own. Though I had had a sage guide in my father, and a supportive mother and twin, I had lacked a stable family unit. The paradox of my broken but loving family made me wish to be a father more than anything in the world.

Clearly, the universe was listening, because in early October, Darnella found out she was pregnant. Nine months later, on July 21, 2019, Bella Angélique Holness was born just a few hours past midnight. Holding her in my arms, I cried tears of joy for the first time in my life. Deep in my heart, I felt my mother's angelic presence bless the arrival of my beautiful daughter.

IT TOOK THE CITY nearly six months to produce the documentation that would serve as a base for the public consultation. But rather than honestly assessing the city's shortcomings and the gaps in municipal services, it produced a public relations package to boast about its tepid inclusion and diversity initiatives. This didn't surprise me. The city could sugarcoat its poor record all it wanted, but it could not silence the hearings that were about to commence.

On the opening day of the consultation, in a hotel conference hall filled with hundreds of people, I spoke about why the petition had been launched and what our mission and vision were. I was passionate. I believed our accomplishment in securing the consultation was similar to those of the civil rights activists I had long admired. I spoke from the heart about the values of community, democracy, and citizenship, and the problems so many Montrealers face daily. I dove into a series of issues, including the economy, housing, policing, culture, urban planning, and the environment, that at the time were either rarely addressed head-on or for which little to no action had been taken to solve. (An example: the boroughs of Montréal-Nord, Rivière-des-Prairies, Saint-Léonard, and Anjou all share one sports center despite having a combined population of more than three hundred thousand.) Thinking back to the heat wave just a few months before, I spoke strongly about environmental discrimination and the impact of climate change on marginalized and vulnerable communities. I highlighted the fact that the city was not taking environmental discrimination seriously and had no emergency plans in place in the event of a disaster. Less than two years later, it would be a health crisis—in the form of the COVID-19 pandemic—that would highlight the city's lack of emergency preparedness. Montréal-Nord, the borough in which I ran during the 2017 election, would become the epicenter of the pandemic in Canada.

The consultation, which brought together more than seven thousand people and three hundred organizations, lasted eighteen months and cost the city upward of $600,000—a small price to pay for years of turning a blind eye to systemic racism. Each testimonial increased my awareness, and that of the other attendees, of shared experiences of marginality across Montreal. Every aspect of public policy would need to be reevaluated. This wouldn't be just difficult; it would require a profound act of imagination.

During the consultation, the OCPM prepared and sent a series of questions to the mayor's office. But the one that I and many others were impatiently awaiting an answer for was whether Montreal's municipal government was willing to recognize systemic racism in the city. On July 2, 2019, in an official response to the OCPM, the mayor's office declared that it *did not* recognize the "systemic" nature of racism and discrimination. The response was steeped in denial. At the time, Black people were four to five times more likely to be stopped by Montreal's police officers. Still today, less than 2 percent of the city's management positions are held by people of color; there are significantly fewer green spaces and sports centers in low-income boroughs with high concentrations of visible minorities; and life expectancy for marginalized people is far lower . . . the list goes on.

We were hopeful, though, that the citizen-led recommendations derived from the consultation would change all of that. The city had at least already committed to establishing a permanent office to implement the recommendations, which were set to be released shortly. That fact alone made me feel that we were making a difference and that each participant in the consultation was showing the city, the country, and even the world, what it meant to stand up for their rights. We weren't demonstrating the power of just one person to make change. We were demonstrating the power of the collective. Of togetherness. Of dedication. Of strife. Of focus. Of hard work. Of a real revolution.

ON MAY 25, 2020, a few days before the recommendations were to be published, and with the COVID-19 pandemic gripping the globe, George Floyd, a forty-six-year-old African American man, was murdered by police officer Derek Chauvin in Minneapolis. Four days later, Chauvin was arrested and charged with the crime. Shortly afterward, a series of antiracism protest marches were organized around the world, including in Montreal.

The death of George Floyd—and of Americans Trayvon Martin, Eric Garner, and Philando Castile, and Canadians Fredy Villanueva and Pierre Coriolan, and many more—showed why I, like many people, had little faith in the US and Canadian criminal justice systems. In March 2021, when Chauvin's trial began, it seemed impossible for justice to be served; after all, there was no bringing George Floyd back. I hoped, at the very least, that justice would be served legally through the conviction of Chauvin.

When the verdict was announced, I was sitting on my couch next to Bella, intently watching the coverage. My jaw dropped as the judge read the jury's decision finding Chauvin guilty on all three counts: unintentional second-degree murder, third-degree murder, and second-degree manslaughter. It was an exception that proved the rule—one of the rare occasions when a white police officer was convicted of killing a Black man. But I was still uneasy. No matter what the judge read aloud, George Floyd's life had still been taken from him. And that would never change.

Much like in the United States, the Black Lives Matter movement in Montreal was vocal after the verdict. Calling for defunding or total abolition of police departments, people marched in the streets. The global community began to take a serious look at police budgets—and so did I. In Montreal's underprivileged boroughs, high-school dropout rates are high, mental health issues surface, and violence ensues—and policing is always prioritized as the solution. Witnessing this firsthand as a teenager, I knew that the crime-and-punishment approach didn't help underserved youth. It infuriated me that policing was seen by Montreal's government—and many others in Canada and around the world—as the only way to ensure the city's "safety." Exactly whose safety, I wondered? Clearly not that of poor brown and Black people. Inspired by the work of so many activists, I knew change was necessary. We had to start investing in people rather than in the police.

BLM's messaging, which was created in solidarity with Indigenous groups, hit home, not just for marginalized social groups, but for everyone around the world. Support for the cause wasn't just local and from people of color, it was global—from those interested in fighting oppression everywhere. It reminded me of the solidarity I had witnessed between races, ethnicities, and religions growing up at the ashram; now it was solidarity among good, socially conscious people fighting against state oppression despite their individual struggles.

AFTER A LENGTHY DELAY, on June 15, 2020, the thirty-eight recommendations from the public consultation were finally released. At 9 a.m. that morning, I stood in front of City Hall to address the dozen or so journalists who had gathered there. I was planning to make a statement about the historic nature of the public-facing document. But, unbeknownst to me, the mayor had strategically held her own press conference thirty minutes earlier so that she could get the first word in. She loftily proclaimed that the time to act was now, and that she would officially recognize the systemic nature of racism in the city, and the role, as mayor, that she could play to combat it. With these simple words, Valérie Plante tried to position herself as a bastion of social change without ever putting in the work and, in my eyes, without ever having the intention to do so. Regardless, journalists ran back to their offices to publish her story, ignoring the fact that it had been 924 days since I had announced the need for concrete action on systemic racism in the city *and* that her government had previously denied the existence of systemic racism in its official response to the OCPM. In that moment, I understood the degree to which politics was about optics and controlling the public discourse. Through political gamesmanship, the mayor positioned herself as a campaigner against systemic racism. But, voluntarily or not, she had now made herself an "ally," and with that came accountability. In that sense, we were moving in the right direction.

Shortly afterward, an article about me appeared in the *New York Times* with the headline "The Man Striving to Be the 'Canadian Obama.'" It was the first time I'd been written about in such a major outlet—and it made a splash. Picking up the story, Canadian television network CTV proposed making a short documentary about my life, and I agreed. As we filmed, they asked about my upbringing, my father, and my journey into politics. Strategically, I avoided talking about my mother. Even up to this day, I speak about my mother as if she was still alive. When people ask me about my parents, or ask where my mother lives, I often say, "Le Plateau," as if I could head up the street and go visit her. It's a painful memory that I rarely expose myself to. It was all going smoothly, and I felt confident about how my family and I were being portrayed. But then the interviewer asked me a question about my brother while we were chatting about police and public security. It caught me off guard.

I paused. Thoughts came rushing to me, including the tumultuous struggles our family, particularly my twin, had been going through. Our bond as twins had always been strong, and now, I couldn't fight back the tears. His situation seemed unsolvable, and it was devastating for me.

So vivid were those challenging moments in my memory that I began to relive my original emotions. With my guard down, my eyes began to water, my lips tensed, and before I knew it, I was crying in front of the cameras. But I wouldn't be embarrassed by being my raw, genuine self.

My story of triumph, empowerment, and vulnerability struck a chord with Canadians, thousands of whom sent me messages and emails after seeing the documentary. One email in particular stood out, though: Helen Hayes, a PhD student at McGill, wrote to thank me for my work and inspiration. Her well-crafted words resonated with me, and although she was a stranger, I somehow felt I could trust her. During our first phone call, we immediately connected, and Helen soon became an important ally in both my community and political work. Among other things, she led a group of ten Montreal in Action researchers drafting an action plan for the consultation's thirty-eight recommendations and wrote a call-to-action to pressure the city to implement them. I'm certain that my intuition about Helen—and so many others who guided and supported my activism—came from my mother. Awakening experiences had taught me the difference between genuine and performative allyship. Helen, though, was the Real McCoy. The connection we forged proved to be a step in the right direction, as big political moves were on the horizon.

THIRTEEN

PURSUIT OF THE
PROMISED LAND

*There comes a time when one must take a position that is
neither safe, nor politic, nor popular, but he must take it
because conscience tells him it is right.*
—Martin Luther King Jr.

By mid-December 2020, seven months after the death of George
Floyd, the global hype around racial justice was abating. Performative black squares and hashtags on social media and "take-a-knee"
protests had resulted in little to no change in our communities.
Police budgets were expanding; cops were still shooting and profiling people of color; unemployment rates in racialized communities
were still well above the national average in both the United States
and Canada; and necessary investments to remedy the health in-

equalities exposed during the pandemic never arrived. I had witnessed the cycle before: a cop kills a Black man, there is outcry in the form of protests and civil disobedience, and then silence, a return to our daily lives as if nothing had ever occurred.

The work on the ground had to continue. I, along with millions of others around the world, remained hungry for lasting change. George Floyd and countless others should not die in vain. After finishing my final law school exam, I was elated—for a few hours at least. I quickly moved on to the next step in my journey. My options were to attend "bar school"—courses that help recent law grads study for the Quebec bar examination—or run for mayor in the upcoming municipal election. I figured that bar school would always be an option, but the election was urgent.

Around the time I was contemplating a run, Verushka Lieutenant-Duval, a part-time professor at the University of Ottawa, was suspended for her use of "n———" in one of her classes. Outraged at what they saw as an infringement of Lieutenant-Duval's rights, major parties in Quebec, and the federal Bloc Québécois, started proposing legislation to protect "academic freedom," or in this case, the right for a professor to say "n———."

From my point of view, the issue was simple: a Quebec government that was openly discriminatory, that was fixated on maintaining white supremacy, was asserting the right of people to say "n———" in academic contexts and beyond. Some teachers found the government's position emboldening. To prove the point that censorship had no place in the classroom and that freedom of expression was without limitations, Vincent Ouellette, a history teacher in Montréal-Nord, repeatedly used the word in his diverse classroom in both French and English, causing a public outcry that eventually led to his suspension.

As Black people, we have attempted to reclaim the term once

used to oppress us by incorporating it into our music, culture, and everyday speech. But n——— did not shed its violent DNA on its path to adoption. It may not be possible to eliminate it from our vocabulary, but as inspired by the writings originated by Paulo Freire, in my view, we are keeping a piece of the oppressor within us every time we use a term that was a tool to debase us, demean us, and rid us of our humanity.

Beyond words, I wanted to flip the script, be a positive role model, and show the younger generation that our intersectional identities are a source of power, not despair. Being Black, being biracial, being multicultural was a source of empowerment, but I wanted to persuade minority youth, and prove it to my city, the province, and the country. I experienced how simply seeing a person that looked like me could set someone on the right track. It was now my turn to give back, to lead, to be a role model for my community. I decided I needed to take my shot at the 2021 election, to show that we could also aim for governance and the halls of power to dissolve divisions in society and build a city that would be inclusive to all.

The 2021 municipal election was dubbed "The Rematch" between the current mayor, Valérie Plante, and the former mayor, Denis Coderre. All other contenders were considered marginal to the storyline. But having been an underdog for so much of my life, I didn't let my outsider status deter me from entering the fray. Mom's passing continued to inspire me. I continued to embody her spirit, her sense of adventure, and her essence. Who knew if I would be alive tomorrow? Life is short, so there was every reason to act now.

I had a vision for Montreal that was beyond politics: I wanted to build a city, a place, that all people could call home. I aspired to make all Montrealers, including the most disenfranchised and dispossessed, feel at home. Achieving that required clear measures:

an economy that worked for everyone; affordable housing; urban planning that would give everyone access to green spaces and infrastructure for leisure, sport, and recreation; quality and affordable public transportation; proper demographic representation in the cultural sphere; freedom of personal expression (including through religious symbols and language); and a city council that reflected Montreal's DNA. I wanted to change the perception of underserved boroughs as being inhabited by undeserving people. I was driven to ride the wave of revolutionary energy that rose up from the movement around the petition for the consultation and crash it into politics, to make civil rights a part of permanent democratic structures. Most important, I wanted human dignity for all, including people of color from whom it had been stripped at every turn. Achieving employment equity and proper representation required securing dignity, respect, and inviolability for all. I was committed to giving the high-sounding dicta in the Canadian Constitution some heft by putting concrete policies in place to ensure them.

My 2017 RUN HAD RESULTED in moral victories. This time around, however, I hoped to increase my chances of winning at the ballot box. Joining an established party would accomplish that, so I began to explore the possibility of joining Denis Coderre's team, who was interested in having me come on board. Coderre was a political heavyweight in the city, and after a few phone calls and a stroll with him around the Old Port, I strongly considered allying with him. The last thing I wanted was to "fail" in another election. Winning a seat on the council would give me political decision-making power and the ability to influence change from within. The problem was that Coderre's policies—on housing, culture, the environment, sports infrastructure, and especially policing—didn't align with mine. In fact, he was as right-wing as the city's politicians came. He proposed, for example, to increase the police budget and the number of officers, all while his hometown borough of Montréal-Nord was still without that infamous sports center. My moral compass was sending me in the opposite direction, despite the lure of financial security and gaining the ability to affect policy.

Dad's advice echoed in my conscience once again: "Don't let your financial situation pressure you to undermine your integrity."

As I grappled with the decision, I took a walk through my neighborhood to people-watch and daydream about my political aspirations and what I really wanted to accomplish with my second campaign. Shortly into my walk, I took a seat on a bench in front of Place des Arts, near the same spot where I'd lost my wallet all those years ago, and a homeless woman approached me to ask me for some change. She was wearing a torn black hoodie and cargo pants. Her hair was knotted, and her teeth were rotten. But her eyes were kind, and her smile was genuine. I gave her the change I had in my pocket, and she went on her way. No more than ten minutes later, though, she approached me again, having clearly forgotten she'd already asked me for money. I calmly nodded and gave her the $10 bill I had in my wallet.

As I was about to get up and walk away, she stuck her hand out toward me.

"Donne-moi ta main. Tu peux me faire confiance" ("Give me your hand. You can trust me"), she said, looking deeply into my eyes. I reluctantly touched her extended index finger to reciprocate.

"Ma mère faisait ça avec moi" ("My mom used to do this with me"), she said.

I smiled.

"J'espère que tu obtiendras tout ce que tu souhaites" ("I hope you get everything you wish for"), she said. She walked away, her feet dragging across the bricks, then stopped and looked back at me.

"Reste égal à toi-même." I had never heard the expression before, but the message was clear: stay true to yourself.

It felt like my mother was giving me another sign. My upbringing was rooted in humanity, justice, and spirituality, and I wasn't about to throw it all away for a paycheck. I grew up in a Montreal that didn't give me access to quality sports or other infrastructure that might have supported me. There were no politicians fighting for kids like me or for people like the woman I had just met. I was inspired to change that reality for the next generation. I wanted to lead a movement with inclusive policies and a vision that reflected my upbringing. This woman was a reminder of those for whom I, and all the other grassroots activists I had worked with, were fighting for: the forgotten, the disenfranchised, the dispossessed.

The poverty and adversity I'd faced had made me resilient, but I'd seen others get crushed by the excessive weight of those circumstances. It was those folks, the ones who dropped through the social safety net, for whom we needed to care and provide a cushion.

It wasn't just about material circumstances, either. I was lucky to have had various guardians and a series of micro-victories shore up my confidence. Some were quotidian, such as walking through bush and bramble to get home from school at the ashram; some had been personally meaningful, like winning the Grey Cup and breaking into McGill's bastion of privilege. As I reflected on the connection between value and values, I saw that my own unwavering values would give me the wings not only to run for mayor, but also to establish a party that would restore dignity to those from underserved boroughs so that they, too, could bring themselves and their values forth into the world.

I thought, too, about how my independent nature was now serving me politically by making me wary of dubious partnerships. It was also putting the fight in me. Yet again, my moral compass pressed upon me, pointing me in the right direction.

My decision started to solidify as I made my way through this personal "experiment in truth." Despite the sense of urgency, it took time, deliberation, and some serendipitous experiences in the external world to recalibrate the dynamic in me between temptation and authenticity, between my head and my heart.

The next morning, I'd made my decision: instead of joining the establishment, I would blaze my own trail. I wouldn't just run for Montreal's mayoralty; I would create a new political party, Movement Montreal. Bolstered by a vision for the future that would highlight the most pressing issues and make everyone feel welcome in our diverse metropolis, I wanted this grassroots start-up to be a true political alternative—the only party representing and advocating for *all* Montrealers, in their beautiful diversity. I hoped to embody the feelings I had when I lived at the ashram—of being carefree and genuinely accepted for who I was—and make them a reality for every person on the island. My vision was to make my city a home for all.

ON THE DAY OF THE ANNOUNCEMENT I felt at peace. Movement Montreal embodied everything that I stood for, that I was fighting for, and that I wanted to build. It was not just about public policy ideas, it was about life. This was an opportunity for me to share a novel social project and vision with my community, my city, my province, and my country.

I walked down to City Hall as calmly as if I were going for coffee with a friend. Behind the scenes, Helen, a key ally, had sent out press releases and created an outline of the party's platform, new social media accounts, and a campaign strategy.

"TODAY IS A BEAUTIFUL DAY on the steps of City Hall. I'm officially announcing the creation of a new party, Movement Montreal, and my candidacy for mayor of Montreal." Journalists scrambled to take notes. Cameras clicked. Microphones drew closer. My voice echoed throughout City Hall's courtyard, the location I had chosen for my announcement.

"We are a grassroots movement that will not just represent Montrealers, but will fight for everyday Montrealers and address their real needs." I spoke with all the conviction I felt in my heart. I was sending a message that Movement Montreal would empower citizens' voices and be the first political party truly to address their core preoccupations. I spoke about renewal and innovation, about how I planned to address inequality, about the fact that twenty-four thousand people were waiting for social housing. I spoke about small businesses and how the pandemic impacted them. I was sharing a holistic vision for an inclusive and prosperous Montreal. After my speech, I was bombarded with questions from reporters:

"Are you the first Black mayoral candidate in Montreal's history?"

"Do you consider yourself to be a Canadian version of Alexandria Ocasio-Cortez?"

"Are you left-leaning or right-leaning?"

All these questions had little or nothing to do with the policies and messaging that I had just shared. Articles popped up in major English and French newspapers, and my press conference was covered by all the city's major media outlets: "Balarama Holness, Athlete and Activist, Announces Mayoral Run," was a main headline.

Later that night, the dust having settled, I began reading articles about the announcement. Montreal's most prominent French paper, *La Presse*, had written that I wanted "to be Montreal's first Black mayor," despite my never mentioning race in any of my public statements. In fact, I made a conscious decision to *not* speak about the possibility of becoming Montreal's "first Black mayor." I was simply vying to be *the* mayor. I was proud of our diversity as a team, and yet I didn't address identity politics because, in that moment, I wanted the media and public to consider the content of our policies, not the color of our skin. We didn't need to highlight our party's diversity because it was a given—just as our city's diversity was a given. Diversity is a sign of a healthy democracy, not a token to be brandished for political expediency, as parties too often do.

THE SUPPORT I RECEIVED in the days following the announcement was overwhelming. Everyday Montrealers, people from all walks of life, sent me messages, greeted me in the streets, and signed up to be volunteers and candidates with the party. Our movement had energy and momentum. Surprisingly, though, Montreal's leading Black journalists and columnists greeted my candidacy with silence. This was not representative of how diverse communities on the ground— Black, Arab, Spanish, or otherwise—greeted my candidacy. My candidacy was beyond race, but those who should have been the loudest supporters hid in silence. It felt like a quieter version of the discord I had experienced when I announced the petition just a few years before.

At the same time, much of the white francophone community was in an uproar. The press conference I gave after the announcement was bilingual, but it began in English, not French, which only meant one thing to francophones: that I was a blasphemous anglophone trying to derail the city's culture and heritage. No one in the francophone press mentioned anything about the substance of my speech, or my ideas for the city; instead, they immediately started taking shots at my identity. It felt like the challenges that I had faced in my personal life were now migrating into my public life. I would simply have to overcome them there as well. And on the ground, I had truly diverse support. Just like the ashram had taught me, I could—and would—overcome obstacles by remaining positive, staying connected to the world and its people, and knowing my path was clear and purposeful.

ON JUNE 3, 2021, we announced our first candidate, Idil Issa, a strong community advocate and leader. Given Idil's experience and leadership at the grassroots level, her candidacy helped bolster Movement Montreal's reach with local community groups.

But Idil was just one of a team of nearly seventy candidates who, collectively speaking, were the most diverse in the city's electoral history. We were Bangladeshi, Syrian, Indian, Somalian, Brazilian, Jamaican, Polish, Salvadoran, Russian, Italian, Moroccan, Mexican, Haitian, and Irish, among other ethnicities. We were also religiously diverse. Muslims, Jews, Christians, and Hindus all came together with a common goal: to represent Montreal and its values. From housing advocates to environmentalists, entrepreneurs, women's rights activists, and lawyers, we had a team that was as motivated as I was to change Montreal. That was the beauty of creating a new political party from the ground up: every person involved could advance the movement in their own unique way, and collectively we could set the example of how representative our democratic institutions should be.

My move to run for mayor was bold, and so were our party's

policies. One of our most ambitious was inspired by a proposal by Boston mayor Michelle Wu: free transit for people twenty-five years old and younger. The free transit policy would align Montreal with global trends, but it was also deeply personal to me. When Jugy and I were young, Mom had to dole out hundreds of dollars a year for us to ride the bus and subway. Getting kids to necessary, everyday places—school, sports venues, family get-togethers—is a serious financial burden for single parents like our mother. I didn't want other parents to have to go through what she had: counting the nickels and dimes for our fares. The policy wouldn't just address climate change by reducing emissions and traffic; it would also put money back in the pockets of Montrealers who were struggling financially.

Later in the campaign, I also brought forth the idea of bringing an NBA team to Montreal. When I was growing up, playing basketball gave me freedom and a sense of belonging. On the campaign trail in 2017, I had felt that way while bonding with youngsters on the court. Becoming an NBA city wouldn't just attract business to Montreal; it could also inspire a new generation of underserved youth. It could give them hope. Even though it was a long shot given the cost associated with a new franchise team, my proposal gave me occasion to discuss youth's relationship to recreation, violence, and mental health—issues that had become particularly salient during the worst of the pandemic. It was also a way to show the youth in Montréal-Nord that I had not forgotten about them. Despite having no sports centers in Montréal-Nord, it was home to NBA stars such as Chris Boucher from the Toronto Raptors, Luguentz Dort from the Oklahoma City Thunder, and Bennedict Mathurin from the Indiana Pacers. Montreal had potential and so did Montréal-Nord. If only we stopped treating these youth like hoodlums, the sky would be the limit.

..

DESPITE THE ONGOING PANDEMIC, on the eve of Quebec's "national" holiday, Saint-Jean-Baptiste Day—or "Saint-Jean," as it's colloquially known—the city was slated to celebrate with parades, parties, and of course fireworks. Sure, I would join in the festivities, but the truth was, like many Montrealers, that I'd never felt the holiday was for me. Maybe it was because, growing up, I had never really felt like a Quebecer. Being neither French nor white, I, and many of my friends and loved ones, didn't fit the mythical "norm" of what it meant to be a Quebecer.

Aiming to hit at the heart of it all and proclaim Quebec *our* home too—home to minorities, immigrants, Indigenous peoples, and anyone and everyone who is seen as "other"—I sent a message to a well-respected journalist suggesting they write a story about another of my proposals: linguistic independence for Montreal. I hoped the city could be, like the country, officially bilingual. For far too long, I'd felt that the government, like a watchful teacher making sure children spoke French in the school hallways, was overstepping. Bilingual status would necessarily put Montreal's French community on equal footing with its anglophone community. I knew that this would be seen as a wild threat to French culture. It would effectively turn my candidacy into a rebellion. As with my application to law school, it would be a way of saying, You can't keep us out of your space, because it's actually *our* space, too. If creating a rebelliously wild campaign would import a few enemies and even hurt my reputation, I was fine with it. I would rather be notorious and respected, fighting for what I believed in, than a stereotypical politician who would say anything to get elected.

The truth is, a majority of Montrealers are fully bilingual, and many are even trilingual. So as rebellious as it might have sounded, my proposal was in many ways a practical reflection of the reality of Montreal in 2021 and beyond. By pure force of demographics, baby boomers, immigration and a low birth rate, Montreal—the whole province and country for that matter—was becoming increasingly multilingual and diverse.

From a young age, I heard, saw, and felt how the beauty of French culture could enrich people. But forcing the language on anglophones and allophones (those whose first language is neither of Canada's official languages) wouldn't make them respect it, or feel welcome in the city. I was determined to use my platform with Movement Montreal to bridge cultural gaps, unite the city, and make Montreal stronger than it had ever been, for everyone. My agenda wasn't to bring French culture "down." Rather, it was to help English-speaking people feel part of the metropolis. At the core, it was about inclusivity and equal rights. It was about the kind of compromise that Mom had encouraged when Jugy and I first met her francophone family.

The debate on language that I pushed into the public space caused an uproar across French- and English-speaking Montreal. Since the city didn't have the jurisdictional right to modify its language status independently of the province, I called on the people of Montreal to decide their linguistic fate. That's right: twenty-six years after Quebec's last referendum, I was calling for another. I sought to take ownership of the very word—*referendum*—that had torn so many Canadians apart in the twentieth century. I knew it would bring up intense feelings for Montrealers who'd lived through the previous referenda and would alter the way the city's youth interacted with their friends and family. My reasoning was simple. If the province could use this legal tool to put forward an exclusivist policy and rupture the fabric of society, then I could use the very same tool to unify society through a more inclusive policy. I wanted to rebrand the referendum as a tool for empowerment, rather than for domination. I wanted to use my parents' early love story as a model for what can flourish when people don't let their language, skin color, or culture limit them. I knew this would embolden my adversaries, but it would also spark the conversation about language and equality that the city so desperately needed. I was willing to press the issue, whether people voted for me or not—which also differentiated me from the other candidates. I was no politician. I was a rebel fighting for my rights, fighting for our rights.

MONTREAL, A MULTICULTURAL AND generally liberal city, is surrounded by a sea of politically conservative, largely white and francophone districts. These surrounding regions, however, consistently elect enough provincial officials to secure a majority government, which allows them to pass laws based on views and beliefs that diverge significantly from those of Montrealers. The city is constantly being restricted by the provincial government, which dictates everything from which language Montrealers can speak to which religious symbols they can wear.

As Quebec's technological and financial powerhouse, Montreal has paved the path for Quebec's economic dominance at the national and international level. Yet when it comes to decision-making, the city doesn't have a seat at the provincial bargaining table. Like all cities in Canada, Montreal is simply, as the Canadian Constitution notes, "a creature of the province" with minimal powers. The province frames Montreal's laws the same way it does the rest of Quebec. The problem, though, is that Montreal is culturally different from the rest of the province. It's economically different. It's socially different. And these differences and Montreal's uniqueness need to be recognized.

Traveling around the world made me realize that Montreal had more in common with the global community than it did with rural

Quebec. It was dynamic, diverse, multicultural, and full of color. The Quebec government wanted to close itself, and Montreal, off from the rest of the world with exclusionary language and anti-religious and anti-immigration policies. Quebec yearned to free itself from Canada; but in my view, Montreal should be able to free itself from Quebec by becoming a special economic zone, a city-state-like metropolis with the autonomy and power to chart its own destiny, much like some of the places I'd visited during my travels. I decided to make this a pillar of my platform. "Montreal needs to have increased powers and coordination to ensure that we promote the interests of our metropolis both locally and abroad," I explained at a press conference. By lobbying the provincial and federal governments to recognize its unique status, and thereby to grant it statelike powers, Montreal could have greater linguistic, financial, and administrative independence while giving its residents a proportional say in provincial decision-making.

"Much like Singapore and Hamburg, which both hold city-state status, Montreal deserves autonomous control over its economic, social, political, and legal landscape," I argued. "This is particularly important in order to better address the linguistic tensions in the city." City-state status, I believed, could be crucial to addressing the city's poverty and its unique immigration, health, and housing issues—issues that could not be addressed by the province's homogeneous National Assembly. It would be a catch-all solution. But it was bold, so it drew lofty criticism, not just in Montreal, but in political circles across Canada. I wasn't dissuaded, however. I knew that Montreal, with the second-largest economy in Canada, needed to take its place within the Canadian federation if it wanted to thrive. My leadership could propel it there. Montreal needed to be the author of its own destiny. But without support from a majority of Montrealers—including the francophone majority—it would be a significant challenge to push this policy forward. Challenges, however, did not deter the scale and scope of our policies. In a first-past-the-post democratic system where the majority takes all, challenges were abundant. It was simply, the name of the game.

Having watched the January 6 insurrection in the United States less than a year before, I knew the power of extremism and political polarization. In the wake of the attack on the US Capitol complex by Trump supporters—which caused panic, rioting, injury, and death—North American democracy felt eerily fragile. The insurrectionists had quite literally broken down the doors of democracy, attempted to undermine the electoral system, and, in doing so, created even deeper political tensions between Democrats and Republicans.

Although in Canada such extremism appears farfetched, in Quebec, its prospect looms close. French nationalists, as I had grown up witnessing, would do anything to "protect" French culture, much as insurrectionists stormed Capitol Hill to "protect" Donald Trump's "dignity," "honor," and status as American president. The 1970 kidnapping of James Cross and murder of Pierre Laporte by the Front de libération du Québec, and the subsequent invocation of the War Measures Act by Prime Minister Pierre Trudeau, which led to mass arrests, shows that Quebec has a history of violent extremism when it comes to cultural politics and policies. The 2022 trucker convoy that brought Ottawa to a standstill showed that US politics are having a ripple effect into Canada. What differentiated that protest from the US insurrection was that the Canadian convoy was largely peaceful. But in both cases the federal government politicized the event for its own political interests. The rise of political extremism in the United States will exacerbate the long-standing violent extremism in Canada, and in both cases, the core is racial nationalism.

..

MEANWHILE, LIKE IN 2017, my personal life became turbulent right in the middle of the election. This time the phone call was from Jugy.

"I need to find somewhere to live," he said, his voice low and somber. Jugy's news saddened me but I was unsurprised. Our mother had been his rock, and her passing had left him without support and human connection, apart from Dad and me. We had drifted apart after she died, and Jugy had sunk deeper into the basement of society. Despite my responsibilities with the election, I felt the urgency to help my brother.

For me, it could not have come at a worse time. Darnella, Bella, and I were moving from a small one-bedroom condo into a larger two-bedroom, but we had a two-month gap between the end of one lease and the beginning of the other. I told Jugy he could stay with me in my one-bedroom condo until he found a new apartment. At that point, it was the only way to keep him off the streets. Darnella and Bella stayed at her brother's place across the street from Bella's daycare. They were all set up, which gave me peace of mind.

I took care of Jugy while we searched for an apartment for him. In less than a week, I found one. I rented a moving van and packed it to the brim with a bed, some clothes, furniture, pots, and pans—everything he needed to be comfortable. Without saying too much, we unloaded the van, set up the bed, and unpacked the boxes. I had done it again: I had come to the rescue. I was at peace since my brother was safe, but all these trials started to weigh heavy on me.

DRIVING THE RENTED VAN down the streets of Montreal to return it, my eyes were tired, my mind was tired, and my body was tired. Of course, my exhaustion was nothing compared with what Jugy was going through. But in this election, I was battling more than just my political opponents.

I'd gotten hate mail for so many years that it no longer fazed me. But the messages I started receiving during this election were of a different order, and they started to get to me. They were frighteningly malicious and spiteful. One called me a n——— and demanded that I kill myself—or else be shot. This was the straw that broke the camel's back. I knew that I couldn't keep it to myself. For my mental health, and for my security, I needed to share the threats with the police, and the public. After hearing about the incident, major papers quoted me as saying, "Je me sens comme Tupac [Shakur], parce que les gens me tirent de partout" ("I feel like Tupac [Shakur], because people are shooting at me from everywhere"). Listening to Tupac's revolutionary lyrics in high school and university inspired me because they were raw, honest, and truthful. If any person, professor, politician, or otherwise listened to the song "Letter to the President" by Tupac and Outlawz, they would get a clear understanding of how marginalized communities were living. Everything from poverty, welfare, unemployment, mental health, broken families, incarceration, and racial profiling to repatriations was outlined. Despite its release in 1999, decades before the COVID-19 pandemic, Tupac rapped, lyrically lamenting on the links between poverty, ghettos, and sickness. Like the churchgoers back in Montréal-Nord in 2017, Pac was aiming his voice to the Lord, not the willfully blind politicians. After all, it was clear to everyone living in poverty that their health was in peril; however, it required a global pandemic in which the epicenter of death were poor neighborhoods for the world to wake up. Inserting Pac into my narrative during the election was my way of saying that revolutionary rappers were more truthful than most politicians, that Pac's lyrics had more substance than most political platforms.

The outpouring of support I received was overwhelming. Francophones and anglophones of all political affiliations left messages wishing me strength. This comforting moment of humanity, however, was fleeting. I still had my naysayers. Some even claimed that I had fabricated the hate mail for my own political gain.

Online hate can breed offline violence, and I was concerned that the death threats would spawn something bigger. With countless news stories about online radicalization, I knew that this was serious. Even if the authors of threats against me didn't act on them, they could inspire others to do so. I contacted the police, who treated the threats as a criminal offense. After months of investigation, the police obtained a search warrant for a house on the outskirts of Montreal, but the computers they seized had already been wiped. They knew it was the individual in the home, but the evidence was limited. The case was closed.

Growing up in a community built on tolerance, trust, and diversity, I was always deeply affected by hatred. I wondered why everyone couldn't just live in harmony; why identity politics factored so strongly into our social interactions; why people couldn't see each other for who they were rather than what they looked like, where they came from, or how much money was in their bank account. There were times during the election, this being one of them, when I wondered how I could truly enact change. It seemed to me like the whole world needed to be turned upside down—or at least that most people needed a new perspective on life.

BUT AS THE CAMPAIGN ADVANCED, we were gaining momentum. Between putting up posters, canvassing door-to-door, holding weekly training sessions for our Movement Montreal team, and taking interviews as often as I could, I wasn't getting a lot of sleep.

I was skipping meals and never had time to talk to anyone about how I was feeling. I was getting worn out. To add to the stress, I wasn't seeing Darnella and Bella as much as I normally did. It felt like we were distant, divided. Was the family I had wanted so badly slipping away? Everything I was fighting for politically, to build a home in Montreal, was fading, ironically, in my own home.

The death threats, the personal and political attacks, and the sense that my family unit was dissipating were wearing me out. With the debates on the horizon, I knew I needed to reground myself, so I went to the temple to see Dad.

"I have a debate . . ." But before I could finish my sentence, he reiterated what he had told me my whole life.

"Solid confidence, personal magnetism, personal presence, effortless effort." He wanted me to take charge without showing too much effort, to be natural. He believed that my presence and aura would communicate my message. Really, it was a summary of the "superior man" talks he had given my whole life. He didn't see the need to debate or argue.

"Let the jackals fight," he said and paused, knowing that I could be confrontational. Then, "Don't let them drag you into it! Go above their heads."

The first debate, the Youth Debate, was organized by a youth-led not-for-profit organization whose goal was to get young people interested in politics. With all the questions provided in advance, and with the rules subject to dialogue rather than debate, it was an opportunity to allow people to get to know the candidates. At one point during the exchanges, the moderator asked Mayor Plante a simple question: "Who among your opponents most embodies the youth of Montreal?"

Mayor Plante smiled before naming herself the best representative, and then turned to me and said, "Balarama, the question of systemic racism is a question that you advanced very well; I have a lot of respect for that question." I was confused. How could my fight against systemic racism be characterized as "youthful"? The mayor, as well as a range of political commentators, used this tactic to pigeonhole me as a single-issue candidate throughout the election. From issues on the environment to addressing social housing and the future of the next generation, I had expressed myself with ease and poise, just like Dad had said. It was on to the next; one down, two more debates to go.

The second French debate had significantly more pressure. It was televised across the province. This wasn't pre-set questions from youth; rather, this was an opportunity to share a full vision across all sectors of public life. Without a notebook or pen in hand, I calmly walked on stage with a single goal: to present a series of pragmatic, forward-thinking, and innovative policy solutions on issues like employment, housing, public security, and the environment. Inclusion in the debates isn't a given; we had to fight for our place, so it was important not to waste this golden opportunity to get Movement Montreal's message across to French voters. I wanted them to know that I cherished and respected French language and culture, despite my desire to make the city officially bilingual— that I didn't see these things as being mutually exclusive. With all the pressure, I felt at ease. From having the support of phenomenal candidates and tens of thousands of Montrealers who signed my petition back in 2018, I knew they were looking to me to express their unresolved grievances and our vision for Montreal. With effortless effort, that is exactly what I did.

After the debate, I went backstage to greet my team who met me with exuberant smiles and cheers. During this election, they were my backbone, my shield and safety net. I was content that I represented them and our party in a solid way. As we listened to the commentary by the French media, my policies and my presence were discredited. I was not surprised, though. To them, I was the antithesis of their version of Quebec: the son of an immigrant; a multicultural, multilingual educated rebel who would not assimilate to their norms and customs. It was water off my back. Time to prepare for the next encounter, the English debate.

The English debate, which was organized by a consortium of Montreal's English-language media organizations, came just a few weeks after the murder of Jannai Dopwell-Bailey, a sixteen-year-old Black student who had been stabbed to death outside of his Côte-des-Neiges high school. The family had called me to express how deeply their values aligned with my vision for the city, how they wished their son, brother, and cousin lived in the Montreal I envisioned; so when the first question of the debate was a video clip of Dopwell-Bailey's family asking how street violence could be prevented, I took the opportunity to share a more humane and compassionate form of public security, despite the fact that it was not a popular policy position. I called for a reallocation of funds ($100 million) away from policing, the budget for which had ballooned to $700 million, while sports, leisure, recreation, and infrastructure funding was severely lacking.

On that stage, everyone could see that I wasn't just a candidate; they saw the rebel in me come out. With Dad's advice out the window, voters watching would certainly feel my frustration and anger in my tone and manner. I was fine with that. I was no Canadian Obama. I was me. My disenchantment, however, was warranted and shared by many Montrealers. For decades, mayors had promised to assist boroughs on the periphery of the city, from housing to sports centers and employment programs, and the help never came. Despite language being outside the jurisdiction of the municipal government, I pushed it front and center in the debate. I also noted that Bill 21, the discriminatory religious law, was, as Martin Luther King Jr. famously said, unjust and therefore no law at all. Regardless of jurisdiction, no government could create a welcoming city by being silent in the face of injustice.

I fought until the last moment, outlining our policies and, most of all, challenging my adversaries, unapologetically calling them out whenever they sidestepped the truth. In my final statement, I showed my vulnerability. Looking right at the camera, I thought about baby Bella, my family, our city, our home. I articulated that Montreal was not just a global metropolis; it was a place we could all call home. Everything had come full circle. From growing up without having the presence of my parents, to trying to form a family of my own, to designing a metropolis for all Montrealers, I laid everything out on the table.

Post-debate, even my harshest media critics declared that I had won. Denis Coderre, a strategic political fox, sensed that I was splitting the vote and shifted the narrative. The headlines read "A Vote for Balarama Is a Vote for Plante." "If Mr. Holness Wasn't There, Denis Coderre Would Be Mayor of Montreal." My un-yielding conviction for truth and accountability during the debate paid off. According to traditional Hindu philosophy, the social hierarchy of a society holds gurus at the top, followed by Kshatriyas or warriors. I am not sure if my performance was reflective of the guru that the swami prophesied, but one thing was certain, I was a warrior, a fighter, someone who could lead by example.

The next morning, I felt relief—like all the unresolved grievances of Montrealers, of immigrants, diverse communities, anglophones and allophones, and even some francophones had finally been heard. This was beyond politics, like it had always been. It was about speaking truth to power, regardless of how popular or unpopular the position. It was about standing up for our collective rights, for being a role model to my daughter and to the next generation. And for recognizing that I was giving people—including myself—hope. Hope for a better future where we could reimagine our lives and re-assemble our social bonds. I was content. I felt like my team and I had capitalized on a unique opportunity to share our collective vision with Montrealers.

THE MOVEMENT MONTREAL CAMPAIGN was about bringing the city together and creating a party that every Montrealer could see themselves reflected in. And that was what we accomplished. On election night, I received 30,235 votes in my bid for mayor, or just over 7 percent—and the party as a whole received more than 95,000 votes. So many Montrealers had put their faith in us, agreed with our policies, and shared our vision for the future. Valerie Plante was reelected and proved to be an ally. The mayor had strategically placed Dominique Ollivier, the former president of the OCPM who oversaw our public consultation on systemic racism and discrimination, in a winning borough and appointed her as the chair of the executive committee. Moreover, Ms. Ollivier was mandated to oversee the implementation of the thirty-eight recommendations from the consultation. Our years of persistent pressure for change were coming to fruition.

THE FINAL EVENT OF THE ELECTION brought together candidates, supporters, friends, and family. As I navigated the room, seeing all the candidates who had courageously jumped into the democratic arena, I felt inspired. A few weeks earlier, a friend,

Ricardo, had pointed me to Theodore Roosevelt's "man in the arena," which would become the essence of my concession speech. I began as follows:

> The first word that comes to mind in this campaign is "victory." We have candidates who, from day one, have stuck to their values. Stuck to their principles. Worked day in and day out to show Montreal what's possible. We were very clear that we want to build a city, a community we can all call home. And the creation and the construction of that home is a long process. Households aren't built overnight. Cities aren't built overnight. Metropolises aren't built overnight. But Movement Montreal is here to stay, and we're just getting started. Movement Montreal fought. It was difficult. We triumphed. There were ups and there were downs, but we rose to the occasion. Being a critic is easy, but the credit belongs to you, the candidates who jumped into the arena, and fought to build a city that we can all call home. So, from the bottom of my heart, I want to congratulate all the candidates who took the leap, who jumped into the arena, who went against all odds, all barriers, and, despite the obstacles, fought and triumphed. Because we advanced public dialogue. We advanced ideals right here in the city about what it means to be an inclusive, international metropolis. What it means to have affordable housing. What it means to have a thriving economy. We advanced these ideas and we should be proud.

The campaign, in the end, wasn't about politically winning. It wasn't about minorities and majorities. It was about belonging by engaging community and enriching democracy. There is value in advancing public dialogue by pushing ideas into the public space, ultimately seeds that will grow and flourish if we continue to nurture them. By knowing that we had changed the landscape and culture of the city, and affected its future governance, my team and I all felt fulfilled. It wasn't so much the outcome that mattered as much as the process itself. After all, equality is more of an unending pursuit than a final destination.

During my concession speech, I was emotional, not because I was disappointed, but because I was profoundly grateful. The election gave me more than I could have ever imagined, and seeing hundreds of people looking back at us, clapping and cheering as we spoke, I knew we had built the home that we were all after. The home I had longed for as a child. The home we all needed to feel safe, and to thrive and prosper.

Winning or losing elections would not determine the nature of my hometown city. As I stood on stage surrounded by my team, I felt at peace, I felt at home. It turns out that the thing I'd been seeking all this time—home—had been inside me. I just needed to be brave enough to see it, to surround myself with candidates, now friends, who felt like family on this long journey toward fairness, equality, and justice.

AFTER THE ELECTION, THINGS calmed down. I was now able to spend quality time with Bella and Darnella, focus on my mental and physical health, and reconnect with my friends and family. I felt reinvigorated. Fatherhood is blissful. For Bella, her birthdays don't feel too special because we treat every day like a birthday. From picnics, to water parks, to apple picking, to road trips, to hopping from one coffee shop and restaurant to another, she allows me to express my love in a simple yet unconditional way that I have never experienced. When I was younger, the warmth I felt when I came home late, my father already in bed, and the food on the stove with a cover on it, was love. My father had a nurturing style and energy that I inherited. The loss of my mother gave me the awareness and urgency to hug and hold Bella with love and passion every day, because I know that these moments are both precious and fleeting. Well beyond activism, law, and politics, my life is dedicated to the next generation, and that begins with my daughter, Bella.

It took me weeks, if not months, to fully grasp the weight of what we had accomplished, and to reflect back on how we collectively inched our city toward equality through democracy and advocacy. The more I thought about it, the more I realized how enriching the process was, and how important we had become to so many Montrealers. Although I was moving more slowly and taking more time for myself and my family, I was also inspired to get back to work.

Six months after the election, I signed a lease on an office space for Movement Montreal, a place for our new political party and candidates, a place we could call home. It would be a place where we could expand our team, our vision, and our goals—and that's exactly what we did.

My mother's energy, everlasting, was pushing me to continue my journey. I have set my sights on my next big goal: a provincial run. I want to expand on the work we have done at the municipal level. More important, nearly a hundred thousand people are counting on my team and I to carry on. The political rebellion has to continue.

CONCLUSION

My journey to an ever-elusive destination continues. My mother continues to guide and inspire me to live my life on the edge, with urgency, as if everything could be taken from me at any moment. Because of her, I remain fearless, endlessly optimistic, and dedicated to building a society whose spirit mirrors the one that was created the moment my mother and father met at that legendary Bob Marley concert.

The thought of the next generation, embodied in my daughter, Bella, also ignites the fire that burns within me—the fire to fight for rights, for equality, for a more just society, and, most important, for a safe, comfortable, and welcoming place we can all call home.

The roots of systemic racism that are so woven into our daily reality derive from colonialism and the era of slavery. If slavery existed today, who would rebel and who would accept the status quo? Who would fight back? Who would be an ally, who would be an abolitionist? Who would be complicit? Those who died as enslaved people did not die in vain; they died for our collective liberation, for our dignity, for our rights, for a more just and humane society.

As I fight the system alongside activists, artists, teachers, lawyers, and others, we need to realize that, just as for our ancestors and their allies, the results of our actions will have a lasting effect on future generations. We are all standing on the shoulders of rebels, abolitionists, and civil rights giants. We cannot be timid in the face of adversity or get blown over by political, social, and cultural winds; the journey must continue, and we all must blaze the trail for future generations.

As we move forward, there needs to be space for us to heal and strengthen our identities, both individual and collective. My spiritual identity was strengthened at the ashram. My cultural and ethnic identities were shaken through assimilation, and then bolstered through my own efforts: the more I evolved, the more I accepted and loved my intersectional self, which empowered me to rebel in my own way. Through education, meditation, and personal reflection, I was able to return to a truer version of myself, and imagine a better version of society.

What will be the legacy of this era? The state of our global community is nothing more than an amalgamation of all the actions we take as individuals. Therefore, each of us must act with historical consciousness and ethical awareness, recognizing that we all contribute to and are accountable for the society we inhabit, as we work to bend the arc of the moral universe toward justice.

ACKNOWLEDGMENTS

Helen Hayes
Anastasia Pomares
Mathieu Léonard
Ricardo Lamour

ABOUT THE AUTHOR

Originally from Montreal, Balarama Holness is an activist, social entrepreneur, and a former defensive back for the Montreal Alouettes, with whom he won the Grey Cup in 2010. He completed his bachelor's of civil law and his juris doctor, with an interest in constitutional law, at McGill University. As a community organizer and activist, he promotes citizen involvement in key issues such as systemic racism, justice, equality, and inclusion. The founder of Movement Montreal, a municipal political party, he recently ran for mayor of Montreal.